TEACHING AND LEARNING DANCE THROUGH

MEANINGFUL GESTURES

By Anabella Lenzu

Library of Congress Control Number: 2024926487

ISBN: 978-0-9894860-2-6
Registration Number: TXu 2-449-562

DEDICATION AND ACKNOWLEDGMENTS

This book is dedicated to my daughter, Fiamma Lenzu-Carroll, who is my light and my hope. I also dedicate this book to the upcoming generation of dancers, choreographers, and teachers.

I invite you to immerse yourself and pursue self-knowledge because without that, we are lost.

I couldn't imagine my life without books.

Without the words and images of the pillars of dance, I never would have left my cocoon; I never would have spread my wings; I never would have given myself the chance. That is why I write: to give others the courage to believe in themselves, the courage to grow.

For me, writing is not so much a pleasure as it is a civic responsibility, and as an educator, my perennial goal is to generate appreciation for and understanding of the arts and of artists.

I thank my husband, Todd, for being my inspiration, my beacon, and my artistic partner, and to my family for all their love and support.

Thanks also to Christina Graybard for her generosity and help with editing this book, to Angela Schöpke Gonzalez for help with organizing the content, to Isabel Webre for the beautiful design, to Steven Heller for his advice and keen eye, to Rathi Varma for the detailed illustrations, to Emelie Hedvall and Andrea Samonilova for the text transcriptions, to Gisela Gamper for her encouragement and inspiration, and to all my students, who push me to be a better person, educator, and artist every day of my life.

Teaching and Learning Dance Through Meaningful Gestures was made possible by generous donations from the following individuals and foundations. Your donations made all the difference. Your faith in my work keeps the flames of my inspiration burning bright!

Benefactor Circle:
Vermont Foundation

Partner Circle:
Lenzu Family, Carroll Family, Christina Graybard, and Ben Lee.

Associate Circle:
Jeremiah Black, Alex Christie, Kathleen Leiner, Kathryn Barnhardt, Gian Marco LoForte, Shawn Rene Graham, Adam Hockman, Patricia Young, Sue Bernhard, Constance Schwarze, and Kisha Marte.

Friend Circle:
Julia Lindpaintner, Diana Carulli, Marjorie Liebman, Francesca Todesco, Rachel Cohen, Ameneh Atai, Lyonel Laverde, Mary Sofianos, Jeanne Swartelé-Wood, Eric D. Walters, Frank Fortino, Silvio Gitter, Bina Altera, David Hubschman & Calogero Salvo, Auguste Olson, Ruth Sergel, Lulu Lolo, Amanda Chesnut, Laura Caparotti, The City Reliquary, David R. Parsons, James Scruggs, David Sampliner, Yana Schnitzler, Christine Dakin, Sangeeta Yesley, Remi Harris, Maria Hochnowski, Haishan Huang, Eugenia Mello, Karen Fragala Smith, Mary Wandrei, Mar Rodriguez, Rachel Cohen/Racoco and Marya Ursin.

Donor Circle: Ray & Khaki Lerer, Jill Sigman.

CONTENTS

INTRODUCTION

Why I'm Writing This Book

Someone asked me recently about this book. Why do I want to give away my secrets as a dance pedagogue for the past 35 years? My answer, I'm not giving away my secrets. There are no secrets. Knowledge needs to be shared. My job is to spread the word so that more people are happy, fewer people suffer injuries, and the dance field advances.

I feel that a strong foundation in technical and artistic education as a dancer and/or performer is the prerequisite to becoming a professional. As a dancer/performer you must know your tools. A sculptor must have a profound knowledge of her materials, such as clay, to be able to manipulate and create with it. If you are a painter you understand color theory at a deep level. You need to know fundamental things about your medium in order to develop your technique. This is not a secret.

Over the years, many of my students around the world have asked me to record my exercises and make them available as online videos or voice recordings. I decided to write a book instead because I want to share underlying principles and fundamentals. This way readers can develop their own methodologies and exercises using their own creativity! I feel strongly that art education must provide tools for people to be independent thinkers.

My pedagogical approach and the exercises I have developed over the years have helped me and many others in their careers, and that is why I'm putting them in a book for teachers, students, and performers to use in ways that best complement their practices.

I also feel that the more we talk about dance pedagogy, the better it becomes. Each teacher has different methodologies and philosophies. They may contrast with mine, but so what? One should embrace opportunities to think about the principles of teaching movement and dance in different ways. A plurality of voices enrich the field!

> *If I had to share one piece of advice—a "secret"—with teachers and students alike, I would say that you must have the courage to do your own thing—the thing that makes sense for you and who you are—and to have the discipline and commitment to implement that decision even if you are scared and are reluctant to do so. You must never stop exploring and never stop asking questions of yourself and others.*

I have a student who dances professionally for a well-known company, and she says she takes my beginner class just to remind herself of the basics. I feel that getting back to the basics of teaching and learning once in a while lets you do a deep house-cleaning, so to speak. It's an opportunity to encounter yourself and then move forward, exploring your origins and motivations.

With this practice of self-reflection, self-discipline, and considered decision-making, I will guide the reader to conduct a "deep cleaning" of unexamined principles and foster a deep understanding of the Art of Movement and Dance.

Both Images: Anabella teaching at Peridance Center, NYC, 2020

Where My Approach Comes From

My approach as a teacher has evolved over the past 35 years, from founding my own dance school in Argentina to teaching in more than 50 private and public institutions on three different continents. As a choreographer, dance theater is a choice and a destination for me at this point in my life.

My personal dance training has been an incorporation of dance history evolving in my own body. My journey led me from folk dances (flamenco and Spanish dance since I was five years old) to ballet, modern, jazz, neoclassical, contemporary, Butoh, dance theater, and performance art.

I came to the United States when I was 23, intending to study classical modern dance. I found that I wasn't satisfied with modern dance because I had the baggage of experiences with another technique. I realized I am not a contemporary dancer or choreographer because I prefer to use a combination of spoken word, strong ballet technique, and the languages of Argentine folk dance and tango. Add to that the Italian folk dance language I learned while living in Italy and working for the Italian Ministry of Culture. I discovered I needed to speak about this personal evolution in my choreography. I started to feel that sometimes I had to be very specific so the characters I created and choreographed for could speak and not just move. As a result, my work pushed me in the direction of dance theater, which became my choice and destination.

In 2006, I found myself in New York City, where I created my dance theater company, and I realized I didn't have training in theater, how to use my voice, and how to include spoken text with movement. I was upset at this deficiency in my training, so through self-discipline I started to read, study, and take workshops in masks, theater, and voice. I called different theater directors and actors with whom I could collaborate and who could train the dancers of my company.

I always had a strong vision, but I wanted to make sure that I was being precise, specifically serving my own choreography ideas. I created Dance Drama Labs in 2013 to offer information and training about voice and acting for dancers who wanted to go on this journey with me. I sought to bridge the gap between dance and theater training.

In 2020, during the pandemic, I created my online Choreographic Mentorship Program, giving aspiring and professional choreographers from all over the world access to a unique educational opportunity via Zoom. Participating artists focused on development of and experimentation with different choreographic techniques, exploration and examination of the individual creative process, artistic brainstorming, feedback on their evolving choreography, how to write about their work, and collaboration with other artists and designers. In this

Both Images: ALDD's 10th Anniversary Performance at the Argentine Consulate in NYC, 2016

program, students explore different choreographic methodologies for live performances as well as for screen dance/video dance. Participants are given time and space online where they can create new works and expand their creative toolboxes.

In my work and in this book, I am primarily interested in teaching movement techniques and understanding the motivation and process behind gestures. I often ask my students, "Why did you perform an empty movement? You are not just an empty glass, a container! What is happening inside you? What about your feelings, your emotions, your imagination, your life experience and ideas?" My motto—and the principle that drives my work—is "Motion Creates Emotion/Emotion Creates Motion." This principle goes hand in hand with François Delsarte's concept that "Every gesture is expressive of something… It is preceded by and given birth by a thought, a feeling, an emotion, a purpose, a design or a motive." I write, choreograph, and teach just as I aim to integrate mind, body, and spirit. I hope that in the works I choreograph, the artists I work with and audiences will find themselves walking in the same direction to integrate mind, body, and spirit.

It's frustrating to be in the position of wanting to choreograph but lacking all the necessary tools. It's like trying to paint without having all the colors you need. Sometimes limitation is good because it makes you create more colors out of the ones you have! But I feel it's ideal to have access to or knowledge of the whole range of colors that you could use. Having a deeper, broader education gives you more tools to make artistic choices as a dancer, teacher, or choreographer. Don't take chances. Make choices!

In my experience, most students in dance education programs, dance conservatories, and universities have significant gaps in their knowledge because the current state of dance is stagnant, partly because it has fewer monetary resources than other art forms, like music and the visual arts. Dance also suffers because it does not have strong intellectual justification on the part of its proponents.

In addition to dance and movement techniques, the fundamental subjects that should be taught in any dance program should include anatomy, dance history, dance criticism, and theater. I am convinced that closing this gap in dance education will spark an era of change.

As dance artists you must take full responsibility for your choices. The ability to trust in yourself—in both your intuition and your training—allows you to make conscious artistic choices when you need to. **You need consciousness so that your artistic choices make sense in your life.**

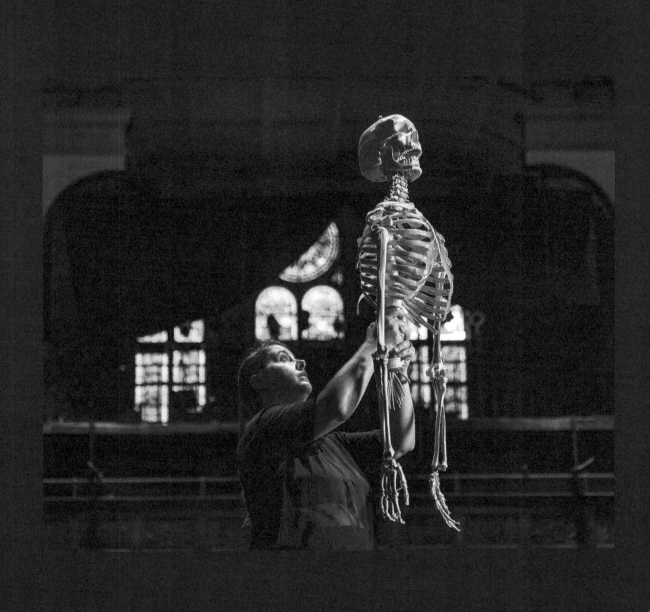

PART I
TEACHING DANCE

Listen to Your Mother, Movement Research at Judson Church, NYC 2023

CHAPTER 1.
OUR RESPONSIBILITY AS DANCE EDUCATORS

I feel that we should teach technique as three things: **as a theory, as a philosophy, and as a practice.** When you study a technique, you study a philosophy or a point of view of life while also studying its practice and application.

Theory

Nobody wants to read about theory! Everyone wants to move, sweat, and feel strong, powerful, sexy, desirable, and liberated by dancing or performing. But for me and many of us, dance is also intellectual. Since my first days as a student in my home town of Bahia Blanca, Argentina, I read about dance because I hungered for knowledge. The dance pioneers in America and Europe—such as Isadora Duncan, Mary Wigman, Doris Humphrey, Martha Graham, Maurice Béjart, and Pina Bausch—ignited the flame of my research.

In my formative years in Argentina, studying the theory of education with pedagogues like Paulo Freire, among others, opened my eyes to a new approach.

Philosophy

I urge you to share a strong point of view—a philosophy—as a teacher. My teachers were always extreme. Russian ballet teachers, Argentine ballet teachers, Brazilians, Americans, Cubans all considered dance their religion. I saw them as very strong and committed artists, and they were not concerned with their polarizing effect. I was able to like them or not like them. I could choose to agree with them or not. It was an important part of my formation as a young performer.

When the choreographer or dance teacher blends too many perspectives or does not have a strong voice, it does not help students find their own voice. I have found that students often define things by contrast. In my family, for example, my father was intensely Catholic (considering priesthood at one point), while my mom was an atheist. Growing up in this environment, it was up to me to decide if I wanted to be Catholic or not. They gave me total freedom to choose. I always heard these two strong opinions in my house and the discussions about them, but all of the discussions were held with deep respect for other points of view. My parents respected each other's viewpoints. So it was up to me to decide the path I wanted to follow. I ended up choosing Catholicism because it made sense to me internally. Perhaps I would have come up with a third approach if neither parent had a strong belief, but for me it really worked that they had strong points of view and respected each other's opinion.

In this way, a teacher or mentor is like a parent. You adopt their ideas, take what they say and move in a different direction, or combine them. It is important to have strong voices to learn from. **We need strong models that we can fight with or against. That is the point of formation of our own artistic voice.** It is that commitment and that strong, identifiable personality that attracted me when I was studying those strong points of view, even if I discovered some were wrong for me. The teachers I studied with had very strong views about life that helped me to find my own voice. They were artists first. They believed in themselves and their missions as artists and educators. Arts gave them self-knowledge. It is important to know yourself in order to take risks in your art. In the end, nothing in art is one hundred percent certain or true. What is the truth, really? It depends on your vantage point.

Practice

I recommend that all dancers, regardless of their dance training, develop technique in part through floor work exercises. We must explore our relationship with gravity and how it affects us. Like a baby learning to walk, one must first build strength and learn how to lift and maintain the head, aligning the spine and the back muscles. With greater strength and focus, a child (and dancer) then needs to learn how to roll over and move to a sitting position, balancing the head over the spine. Finally, we transition to crawl, stand, and attempt to walk. Combining floor, barre, and center work is necessary to better understand the fundamental use of the body from first principles. Sometimes we need to spend more time at the barre. Sometimes we need to spend more time on the floor. Sometimes we just need to spend time in the center. A good teacher knows how and when to develop the aspects of each student's technique.

Dance technique is a closed, structured system, a code, a language by which movement and principles are codified. Everything has a coherent reason. For example: Ballet Technique.

What is style in dance? We can think of style as a dialect, similar to slang, a mix of languages and concepts that do not necessarily match with each other. It's an amalgamation of concepts without an underlying philosophical point of view. For example: Vaganova style (originally from Russia) or Cecchetti style in ballet (originally from Italy).

A dance class is a laboratory for ideas and for examining the functionality of basic principles. It is an opportunity to probe and test the real point of departure. It is essential to employ technical concepts as we explore structure, principles, and fundamentals. A class must follow a structured program or syllabus, even if it is an open studio class. The teacher needs a goal, even if it must be changed according to who shows up to class. A teacher needs to know the class material, the craft that makes it possible, and what can help students become dancers or performers.

As a teacher, you are responsible first and foremost for your work as a pedagogue, not as a choreographer. Many choreographers use class as a kind of practice, reinforcing or experimenting with their choreography. I agree with this approach only if the class is for advanced students. Beginners and intermediate students need a solid foundation in technique in order to process and advance technically and artistically.

A technique class has specific goals. Although it is understandable that a beginner would want to learn how to quickly pick up choreography, such proficiency is useless if the dancer

Fiamma Lenzu-Carroll & Anabella, Rehearsal at La Mama Great Jones Studios, NYC, 2024

lacks proper technique. By contrast, classes that are structured as warm-up followed by a direct jump into a choreographic combination are best suited for professional dancers who want to prepare for auditions or to learn how to quickly pick up choreography. This kind of class should be taken by professional dancers getting ready to perform or by a company preparing for rehearsal.

It is imperative for students' safety and awareness that they understand the differences between laboratories, workshops, master classes, classes and rehearsals.

ALDD Rehearsal at DMAC, NYC, 2016

- **Classes:** Can be open or closed, depending on the institution or program. The length could be from 45 minutes to 2 hours.
- **Master Class:** One-time opportunity to take class with someone special like a well-known and respected teacher, artist, or choreographer who does not teach regular classes. A master class is usually longer than a regular class and often involves demonstrations. Such classes can present a panorama of techniques or styles or they can focus on a specific subject or theme.
- **Workshop:** Can last from 2 days to months. It is an intensive and specific investigation of a topic or topics. Some workshops culminate with an informal or formal presentation of the material learned during the workshop.
- **Laboratories:** A week-, month-, or year-long encounter during which you research a specific topic or topics. Labs are usually guided by a peer, or moderator or facilitator, and the structure is democratic, as they are not held by a teacher or leader. It is like a science lab in which artistic practices are tested.
- **Rehearsals:** Encounters of a group or company whose ultimate goal is to explore, test, and/or perform specific material.

Teaching technique is like preparing a full nutritious dinner, not just the dessert of choreography. Everyone wants to perform choreography, but are they ready? Have they eaten their nutritious dinner?

Maybe they haven't learned how to use the floor yet, so when they roll on the floor they injure or bruise their knees, hips, and spine. Have they learned about gravity or how to fall architecturally? Without a full understanding of the fundamental principles, they are likely to use inappropriate muscle groups and will always be working in what I call "emergency mode" without having all the technical tools to solve movement problems as a dancer. There is great pressure to learn choreography at all costs despite the significant health hazards for an untrained dancer.

And now a special note for teachers, especially if you are someone's first dance teacher. You are responsible for teaching the ethical responsibilities of being a dance professional.

- Respect yourself, your teachers, your peers, and the environment where you work.
- Support one another during the learning process.
- Respect and tolerate different opinions and points of view.

Anabella teaching at Peridance Center, NYC, 2024

Students are ostensibly in class to learn the craft of organizing a body in time and space, but they are also building skills of how to see the world. That is why I make my college students observe class and take notes even when they are sick (provided they don't have a fever). Students can learn by observing. I often hear them saying "Oh, that's how it should look!"

> *Learning a craft is both an inward and an outward*
> *practice. It is important to be able to differentiate elements*
> *of dance and movement with a critical eye.*

It is not only creating a beautiful line with a leg or foot. It is about the execution. It is better to execute one good pirouette than three horrible ones. **Quality, not quantity!**

CHAPTER 2.
UNDERSTANDING THE BODY:
MIND, PHYSIQUE, AND SPIRIT

Maurice Béjart illustrates the concept of flexibility and the strength of vulnerability that has been very important to me over the years. He says that a dancer is at the same time a nun and a boxer—that we must embody those two extremes. The nun inside us connects with the spiritual component of our dancing, and the boxer with the aggressiveness and physical component. That dichotomy also represents the connection we strive for between strength and flexibility of our mind, body, and spirit.

I say that flexibility and strength are two sides of the same coin. When I talk about flexibility and strength, I refer to the flexibility and strength of mind, body and spirit all at the same time. As teachers, we want to create intelligent bodies instead of bodies trained like dogs to obey. We train dogs to sit, stand up, give us their paws, and pretend to be dead. Likewise, so many dancers are trained to do jumps and pirouettes! Our training needs to be intelligent in order to educate both the mind and the body. As Anna Halprin says, "The mind informs the body and the body informs the mind." Our job as teachers is to create smart and intelligent dancers who can be flexible and adaptable in their minds, bodies, and spirits.

According to merriam-webster.com:

> **Catharsis**
> 1a: purification or purgation of the emotions (such as pity and fear) primarily through art
> 1b: a purification or purgation that brings about spiritual renewal or release from tension
> 2: elimination of a complex by bringing it to consciousness and affording it expression

Another concept to explore is vulnerability and its relationship to mental strength and flexibility. We know that our goal is to communicate and produce catharsis in our audiences and to engage in a deep dialogue about humanity with the spectators. We know that working on our strength, flexibility, and imagination will prepare us to be vulnerable, not to be superheroes. We know that we are the subjects of the audience, that we are mirrors of the audience and vice versa. The audience has the power to destroy us or to interest us or to elevate us. Sometimes we have an audience that is made up of dancers, and sometimes we have an audience that knows nothing about dance. Regardless, they're watching you. You are exposed, you are naked, you are open. You are vulnerable. The dance and the dancer are inseparable! You are not an artist who creates and displays a painting or sculpture that exists outside of the artist. As dancers, we are the work of art, the object itself. So, we need to prepare ourselves to be in this vulnerable state, and we must be fully aware that we are the messenger, not the message to give to the audience. To succeed as messengers we need mental, physical, and spiritual strength and flexibility.

Let's talk now about spiritual strength and flexibility. Here in the United States, people are scared to talk about the spirit. I feel strongly that physical exercise is always a spiritual exercise. We cannot separate our minds from our bodies or our spirits. Performing brings us to another level of consciousness. Otherwise there is no point!

What Is the Spirit/Anima/Alma in the Context of Dance?

Many times people associate spirit with ideas of religion or spirituality, but it is something else for us as dancers. Let's call it anima or alma for our purposes to avoid confusion with conventional ideas of the spirit. I feel that this anima or alma moves before the mind and body do. It moves even before the intention to move develops in the mind and before the body realizes it and actually moves.

The anima or alma creates the intention to move, which motivates a physical movement, which in turn becomes energy that passes through the space and then resonates with the alma of a spectator. Each movement is an entire journey from alma to alma, from the spirit of the performer to the spirit of the spectator. This concept has always been there in dance. I am not aware of anyone having spoken about it at length, but teacher Eugenio Barba and director

"Listen to Your Mother" performance at La Mama Moves Festival, NYC, 2024

Nicola Savarese investigate this concept in their book *Dictionary of Theatre Anthropology: The Secret Art of the Performer*, in which they note that "Acquiring consciousness about this topic is the road to being an artist. Without this journey the dancers/performers just will skim the surface."

What Is the Difference Between Spirit/Anima/Alma and Emotion?

It is a blurred line, and sometimes it's difficult to understand. Some choreographers prefer not to delve into emotional exploration in their work or even talk about it. Remember that all different techniques have different perspectives. But in my experience, motion creates emotion and emotion creates motion in both the dancer and the audience.

What can we say about where this movement comes from? What is your center of energy? How do we define the center of energy? If I view the body in a certain way and tell you that your center of movement and energy is your heart or your heart chakra, it would be completely different from me saying that your center of movement is your lungs or your spine! It would change the energy with which you move—and thus your emotions. When the anima or energy of life passes through your center, you will feel something—an emotion. This emotion may or may not be transmitted to the audience. It depends on your technical control and awareness as a dancer/performer. Sometimes, I tell my own dancers not to show or reveal to the audience their emotional states during certain moments of my choreography, but we still work on energy and on projecting that energy. We must always remember that motion creates emotion and that emotion is different from energy.

To be fair, this way of working is particular to dance theater work. Artists who take this approach include Anna Sokolow, Delsarte, and myself. Dance theater asks about the anima, the motivation, and the inspiration for movement, or what we can call pre-movement. Is it emotional, physiological, and physical? It is much more than training your abductors and deep rotator muscles. At the same time, we need to start from something that is tangible to arrive at an intangible thing. So we start with the first thing that we know: the body, our physical container. The body is the container, the door to other levels of consciousness. However, there isn't enough time in a one- or two-hour class to work on all these things. That is why we make the long-term commitment to study theory, philosophy, point of view, and training in technique before approaching different styles of dance or performance modes.

These ideas are also the source of the title of this book, *Teaching and Learning Dance Through Meaningful Gestures*:

> *Inner Thought and Outward Expression. Inner thought*
> *is the engine, the motivation to achieve outward expression that*
> *takes the form of meaningful gestures and movements. My intention is*
> *for this book to open up conversations about these ideas*
> *among different techniques and approaches.*

For this reason, you'll find dispersed throughout the book passages from different theater directors and choreographers that will help us look at these ideas with open minds, bodies, and spirit.

Catharsis in My Own Choreographic Works

> *For me, dance is a prayer and invocation. My art goes hand*
> *in hand with love. I use the body as a receptacle and messenger*
> *of the multiple realities that we are immersed in, and I use art as a tool*
> *to examine identity. It takes courage to reveal intimacy. I frame impulses*
> *of freedom. My work bridges the gap between silence and speech,*
> *between nature and culture, and among mind, body, and spirit.*

My commitment as choreographer and dancer is to stimulate and encourage audiences to identify with the characters and undergo a catharsis of their own impulses and desires, removing the fourth wall that separates artist from audience. The search for the essential drama is transparent so that the audience is wholly involved in the transformative process. Both the dancers and the audience fuse in a psychological and emotional experience. I am creating a vocabulary of meaningful movement that springs directly from emotions with visceral strength. I organize layers of character-driven drama, and I break apart quotidian social gestures. I research and use strong visual aesthetics as portals to open new views to other worlds.

"Listen to Your Mother" performance at La Mama Moves Festival, NYC, 2024

I use movement as portals, as icons, as symbols, and as keys to enter into other states of transformation. I use masks and props as doorways and as mirrors that reflect identity. I inhabit and project a feminine vision of the world—honestly, naturally, and humbly. I use movement, voice, sounds, music, photographs, drawings, and video projections to evoke histories. I am interested in provoking a cathartic experience for the audience in an intimate dialogue. My works are a ceremony of awareness. My works are rituals and documentations of intimacy.

19

Top Left: "No More Beautiful Dances" performance at Exponential Festival at The Brick, Brooklyn, 2019
Middle Left: Anabella teaching at Peridance Center, NYC, 2020
Bottom Left: "No More Beautiful Dances" rehearsal at Center for Performance Research, Brooklyn, 2017
Middle Right: Anabella teaching at Peridance Center, NYC, 2020

CHAPTER 3.
UNDERSTANDING YOURSELF AS A TEACHER

Your Intention Behind Teaching

Before beginning to teach and all throughout your teaching career, it is important to understand why it is you're teaching at all. Why do you want to teach dance and to whom? Before anything else, you need to identify the ultimate goals of your teaching. You must establish your objectives in the context of your life, your students, and your community. Your goals may be personally oriented. For example, "I want everyone in my small community to have access to and enjoy and discover the joy of dance through teaching modern jazz" or "I want to promote the culture and identity of Argentine culture by teaching Argentine tango to Latin communities in my city."

Your goals become realized through conversations about your intentions—about where you are, the nature of the community, and the character and expectations of the people who take class. You will adjust your goals to reflect what you learn from these conversations, and these are the goals you will realize.

How can teachers identify why they want to teach? I strongly suggest keeping a journal and writing daily about this topic. Also, maintain conversations with your friends, family, and mentors, exchanging thoughts about your choice to teach. The next step is to make a plan to get from where you are to realizing your goals.

Once you have your goals and you have your plan, then start writing the content, the program, the syllabus. Remember that the program content and syllabus are a roadmap and help with preparation, but they do not mean classes will go exactly according to your plan. What do you need to achieve your objectives? Do you have a support system? To achieve any kind of success, you must be able to articulate your needs: economical, emotional, psychological, etc. Then comes the time for writing what you plan to teach. Are you teaching technique, a style, improvisation? Are you teaching composition class or theory? Who are your students? Who are the community members? What type of institution are you serving? How long will you be teaching this specific class and group? How many hours per week will the students have your instruction? How many hours of homework will you give them? How will you measure the success of the class, of your students? How will they evaluate it? All of these questions must be carefully considered before moving ahead. Nothing is generic, and there are no recipes for good answers. Everything is specific.

Once all of this is deeply thought through in detail, you will proceed to write your course syllabus. To see examples of my syllabi, go to PART III: TEACHER RESOURCES, page 173, where you will find examples for both theoretical and practical classes I've taught in the past.

You must have an open mind to be able to adapt your strategy while on your journey. Always remember that teaching is linked to service. The term "service in dance" is in decay, but as modern dance pioneer Mary Wigman said in a letter to a young dancer, "Our task lies in serving: to serve the dance, to serve the work, to serve man and to serve life. Keep the artistic fire from being extinguished." I say keep the flame of service in dance for the community.

I compare teaching with parenting. In parenting, it's the listening, the conversations, the innate personalities of the child and the parents that shape the child's personality and allow it to flourish with minimal suppression or restriction.

I believe there are too few conversations among dance teachers about what it means to be a good teacher and how each teacher can approach the same challenges in a classroom. It follows that there are too few conversations about what teachers themselves are learning. Excellent dancers often become teachers, but being a good dancer doesn't mean that you will become a good teacher. Good teaching requires being responsible for other people—other bodies different from your own—to guide them in this journey of self-discovery and self-construction. It requires having a heart full of generosity and compassion, an open eye to see beyond the surface of things, and a quick mind to solve problems and plan strategies. As with being a parent, there is no book or map to guide you in this process. You learn by doing and, crucially, by meditating and reflecting on it.

Also, there are not enough conversations among professionals discussing different methodologies of teaching dance. It is not just about how to prepare the class, how to select the material, or how to do a warm-up, which are important but superficial. We need ongoing conversations with other dance teachers, as well as self-reflection, as we examine the why of teaching!

> *For me, my job as a teacher and mentor is to help my students to think*
> *for themselves, because, as Bell Hooks states, "Education is the practice of freedom."*
> *In teaching, I emphasize critical thinking and personal life experience as it relates*
> *to dance. Wherever I go, I teach with a human and comprehensive pedagogy*
> *in which creativity, ethics, and aesthetics are intertwined.*

Before we explore other issues, let us take a moment to digest some vocabulary that is a key to future discussions.

According to merriam-webster.com:

Pedagogy: the art, science, or profession of teaching
Author's Note: This word might be translated literally as "child-leader." The origin of the English word pedagogue is the Greek *paidagōgos*. It is now a name for a person who leads children by teaching them.

Methodology: a body of methods, rules, and postulates employed by a discipline; a particular procedure or set of procedures

Didactic:
1a: designed or intended to teach
1b: intended to convey instruction and information in addition to serving another purpose (such as pleasure and entertainment)
2: **usually disapproving:** making moral observations : intended to teach proper or moral behavior
Author's Note: Didaktikós is a Greek word that means "apt at teaching." It comes from *didáskein*, meaning "to teach." Something didactic does just that: it teaches or instructs. "Didactic" conveyed a neutral meaning when it was first used in the 17th century and it still does; a didactic piece of writing is one that is meant to be instructive as well as artistic. Parables are generally didactic because they aim to teach a moral lesson. "Didactic" now sometimes has a negative connotation as something that is overburdened with instruction to the point of being dull. Or it might be pompously instructive or moralistic.

Three other words that are fundamental in our lexicon—*education, teaching,* and *training*—are radically different concepts. You need to decide what type of teaching you are dedicated to.

According to merriam-webster.com:

Education:
1a: the action or process of educating or of being educated; also: a stage of such a process
1b: the knowledge and development resulting from the process of being educated
2: the field of study that deals mainly with methods of teaching and learning in schools

Teaching
Noun:
1: the act, practice, or profession of a teacher
2: something taught
Adjective:
of, relating to, used for, or engaged in teaching
Author's Note: Teaching refers to ideas or principles taught by an authority and can apply to becoming accustomed to some action or attitude. We teach students to think for themselves; impart knowledge; instruct by precept, example, or experience that are made known and accepted. Teaching applies to any manner of imparting information or skill so that others may learn.

Instruction
1: to give knowledge to
2: to provide with authoritative information or advice
3: to give an order or command to
Author's Note: Instruction suggests methodical or formal teaching.

Training:
1a: the act, process, or method of one that trains
1b: the skill, knowledge, or experience acquired by one that trains
2: the state of being trained
Author's Note: This word stresses instruction and drill with a specific objective in view—to make one fit, qualified, or proficient; to form by instruction, discipline, or drill; to prepare for a test of skill.

Now that we have looked at the definitions and understand the lexicon in general terms, let me explain my personal points of view on these matters:

- Education in art and in dance is holistic.
- An educator's focus is the holistic integration of the development of the mind, body, and morals/ethics.
- Education is risky because we think about the future and how as educators we help individuals combine the creation of their identity as artists with the culture where the individual belongs or is immersed in, as well as the historical context of the world and the history of art. We challenge students to find their own voices and understand their roles in society as artists and art practitioners.
- Education introduces the student to the meaning of their entire world.
- Education is waking the individual to confront the future and to their responsibility to identify their motivations. I'm in a position to help them address why dance is their best tool for this endeavor.

- Education integrates the heart, spirit, and mind.
- The central goal of education is freedom—intellectual, artistic, spiritual, physical.
- Education is a beginning or resetting that changes an individual. It solidifies new voices and ideas. Innovation is impossible without knowledge of the individual's history and that of the wider world.
- Education empowers the individual to be an agent of change.
- Education challenges the status quo and enables us to learn from the past.
- Dance education has been suffering lately because performers are not taught how to integrate mind, body, and spirit.
- Education presents a total reality, where how and why are integrated, and the human experience is enriched.
- Education must provide tools for critical analysis of the present to create a better future.
- Education must focus on values, gratitude, respect, and coherency.
- Education must awaken curiosity and increase the thirst for knowledge.

Regarding the teaching and training definitions cited above, educators are just passing down the skills and the formalities of teaching methods, but they typically don't adapt their methods to how their individual students live and work, nor do they offer any holistic integration. They focus only on results, not on the process. Teaching and training are two components of education, but this is just the beginning. For example, suppose a performer's trained body can only demonstrate skills and tricks. Further training is needed for him to develop a critical mind or mind and body will be cruelly divided. To be effective, teaching methods must always adapt to different generations and cultures.

The Difference Between Methodology and Pedagogy

Pedagogy is a discipline that deals with the theory and practice of education. It informs teaching strategies, teacher actions, and teacher judgments and decisions by taking into consideration theories of learning, understanding of students and their needs, and the backgrounds and interests of individual students.

Methodology is the systematic, theoretical analysis of the methods applied to a field of study. It encompasses concepts such as paradigms, theoretical models, phases, and quantitative or qualitative techniques. A methodology does not set out to provide solutions so it is not the same as a method. A methodology offers the theoretical underpinning for understanding which method, set of methods, or best practices can be applied to a specific case.

Left Page:
Anabella teaching at Peridance Center, NYC, 2019

Right Page:
Top: Anabella teaching at Peridance Center, NYC, 2024
Middle: Anabella teaching at Peridance Center, NYC, 2020
Bottom: *Unveiling Motion and Emotion* book lecture at Institute Cervantes, NYC, 2014

Continuing Self-Education as a Teacher

As a teacher, it is your responsibility to continually revisit, develop, and question your approach as you learn from your students and context. I love to share with my students something that challenges the way I've always taught previously and how my thinking has changed. Your teaching must change and adapt all the time with each student. Who knows? In a few years I may have changed my mind about the ideas in this book!

We change everyday as we adapt to the world that has evolved around you. For me, practicing my art is a continuous process of asking questions, challenging the status quo, and adapting to different circumstances in my life and my students' lives. If you stop asking yourself questions, you die inside. If you don't have doubts, if you stop your search, there is no action. Doubt and questions are the fuel of life.

For me, being an artist is about continuing the internal conversation about who I am, how I perceive the world, and how I can serve and contribute to a better world.

Several years ago, I taught a methodology of teaching workshop in NYC, and what unfolded during those sessions was remarkable. I asked the participants—all of whom were teachers—to do a writing exercise, enumerating things that they loved and things that they hated about teachers they had throughout their lives—not just in dance but across all fields. Among many insights, one shared concern was why we teachers repeat the mistakes that our former teachers made or why we teach the opposite without deep consideration?

I love reading autobiographies by dancers/performers and choreographers to understand their private lives in relation to the development of their artistic careers. I find it valuable to understand their choices and the circumstances that inspired or limited them and their creative processes. Here are the names of a few of the books that I revisit often and that explore these issues:

Isadora Duncan, *My Life*
Doris Humphrey, *An Artist First*
Martha Graham, *Blood Memory*
Anna Sokolow, *A Rebellious Spirit*
Eric Hawkins, *The Body Is a Clear Place*
Maurice Béjart, *Un Instante en la Vida Ajena*
Elizabeth Streb, *How to Become an Action Hero*
Kazuo Ohno, *From Without and Within*
Anna Halprin, *Moving Toward Life*
Twyla Tharp, *The Creative Habit*

Some of these artists' approaches resonate with me and some do not. For example, I love the way Elizabeth Streb analyzes different forces that affect movements/action of the body in space. I greatly enjoy reading her ideas and point of view about action, but I will never develop a similar aesthetic because I am a different person with a different background.

The more I teach and the more I study, I either reinforce or revise my theories. My experience doesn't come only from the theoretical. It also comes from my ongoing experiences as a teacher and choreographer. Having these frames of reference allows me to be who I am as an artist and teacher. How can I teach dance if I am not an active artist?

I lead by example. The act of teaching teaches students an essential part of the creative process.

Left: ALDD's 10th Anniversary Performance at the Argentine Consulate in NYC, 2016
Right: *Unveiling Motion and Emotion* book lecture at Institute Cervantes, NYC, 2014

The Mind of the Beginner, The Mind of the Expert

The following quotations are from *Zen Mind, Beginner's Mind, Informal Talks on Zen Meditation and Practice* by Shunryu Suzuki.

"I am interested in helping you keep your practice from becoming impure. In Japan, we have a phrase *shoshin*, which means beginner's mind. The goal of practice is always to keep your beginner's mind."

When you are learning an important text, Suzuki asks "...but what will happen to you if you recite it twice, three times, four times or more? You might easily lose your original attitude towards it."

"This [beginner's mind] does not mean a closed mind, but actually an empty mind and a ready mind. If your mind is empty, it is always ready for anything; it is open to everything; in the beginner's mind there are many possibilities, but in the expert's mind there are few. "

"The beginner's mind is the mind of compassion. When your mind is compassionate, it is boundless."

"Then we are always true to ourselves, in sympathy with all beings, and can actually practice. ...This is also a real secret of the arts: always be a beginner."

Why do I cite these statements about Zen meditation? How did this practice influence my philosophy? I consider the practice of any art a meditation on life. I dedicate my life to investigating the interior logic of performance and the role of the dancer in our culture today, using the five *Ws* and one *H*: who, what, when, where, why, and how. My practice for 30 years has been teaching, choreographing, dancing, and writing.

Nothing fulfills me more than to discover different processes of creation, becoming, and transformation. My curious mind and heart always lead me to a fresh beginning, where creativity helps me to transcend ideas and rules to create meaningful methods. In each new adventure, I'm creating a scene, a show, an education program, or a class. But how does one keep this boundless attitude after 30 years? There are periods when my inner child is fully awake and my discoveries are easy to communicate and generously share with others. There are also periods when the candle is only half lit, and that's when my experience, practice, and mastery of craft guide me like a blind person. It's a precarious balance between my outer and inner states.

Dance is a union with ourselves, with others, and
with our environment. I celebrate, respond, protest, scream, cry,
and laugh about life through dance.

I don't want to follow a formula or lean too heavily on my previous failures and successes. I have a need to keep it fresh, to surprise myself with each discovery. Perhaps unconsciously, I want to remain naive and keep my practice pure, as the master teacher Shunryu Suzuki said.

But what about the mind of the expert? You might think that I consider myself a master after 30 years of teaching in more than 50 institutions on three continents! All I know is that I am here, every day, opening myself to magical and mysterious encounters with others in life, on the stage, and in the classroom.

My daily meditation is observing the bodies of my dancers and students in fine detail, watching with love as their mental, emotional, and spiritual expressions emanate and emerge. They flourish in each rehearsal, in each class. It's like nature revealing itself before your eyes, like a plant growing from a seed and becoming a tree with flowers and fruits. What a privilege! Here is the beginner's mind: observing, nurturing, and guiding others like a gardener because our bodies are a perfect manifestation of life.

When I perform, I feel the forces of life in my entire being. I am more awake and alert, and all my senses are enhanced, ready to share the gift of my dance, ready to connect with others, from *anima* to *anima*. The meditation happens after the show, when I reflect on the interaction between the audience and myself and our reactions. For me, performing is an attempt to have communion with others and with my environment. Perhaps one of our needs as human beings is to connect with the presence of a greater power than ourselves. Sometimes I feel that my dance is a prayer.

I firmly believe a good teacher is an excellent student because they want to remain open to everything and available to new experiences. My profession allows me to experience generosity, compassion, altruism, empathy, tolerance, patience, and gratitude. I value respect and love for others, and I receive it in return when I give myself totally to the learning process.

The art of teaching is about contemplation, appreciation, reflection, exchange, detailed observance, assimilation, and developing a deeper human consciousness. I am humbled, grateful, and thankful for every student, dancer, artist, collaborator, institution, and organization that lets me share my point of view.

Top Left: Anabella teaching at the Peridance Center, NYC, 2018, Top Right: ALDD Rehearsal at DMAC, NYC, 2016
Bottom Left: Anabella teaching at Columbia University, NYC, 2019, Bottom Right: Anabella teaching at Culture Hub, NYC, 2018

CHAPTER 4.
UNDERSTANDING YOUR STUDENTS

To be able to teach, you must know your students. You must understand why they've come to your class, where they're coming from, what they want to do with their lives, and what their issues and goals are.

I remember being in New York City on September 11, 2001. I was at that time a student at Peridance. After September 11, we didn't have class for a week. When we finally returned to class, I remember taking Humphrey-Limón technique with my teacher Jim May. I couldn't lift my arms in class, I could not look up without crying. I was so scared and sad. We all cried several times during class. In response to the emotional and physical heaviness we all brought with us, our teacher changed the class to meet us where we were at that moment. He didn't cancel class, because although we were devastated, we needed to be in a community that embraced us. He knew his students, and we knew him, so he was able to serve us as our teacher and change the repertory and improvisation that we studied. He served us and we supported him.

Knowing your students helps you plan and prepare for your class so you can show up ready for the class to take its own course. You always need to have a plan, a map, but in reality your goal is to serve each individual student, so you need to be ready to take a detour sometimes. Most of the time, I prepare for a class and end up changing my strategy because of students' needs.

Another anecdote: It was the first week of classes in the fall semester at a university in New York City. I was teaching an intermediate level ballet class for junior year students at 8:00 a.m. Suddenly, 10 minutes after class began, a student passed out, fell on the floor, hit his head, and covered the floor with blood. He fainted because he hadn't eaten breakfast and hadn't had enough sleep. We called 911 and the university nurse, and in less than 5 minutes, the student was being treated and was taken to the hospital. Things happen, but how was I to teach the rest of the class? How was I to support the rest of the students? Teachers need to know how to react, how to respond. I feel the key is practice and common sense. The more time you spend in front of a class and get to know each individual, the more tools you have to react appropriately.

Each student is different, and they were shocked after this episode. Some were shaken, and some felt extremely tired. There is no right answer about how to react as a

Top: Anabella teaching at Peridance Center, NYC, 2018
Bottom: Anabella teaching at Peridance Center, NYC, 2019

teacher, but understanding your students is the first step in making sure you meet them where they are and can guide them from there.

As teachers we don't know what will happen in the future. You are in the present moment, addressing issues, helping your students become the best versions of themselves. **We have to create a safe, supportive, and creative environment in which our students can face their psychological or emotional barriers and gain freedom.**

As we seek to understand our students, there are a few teaching goals that I feel are helpful to keep in mind. These goals are:

1. Discover the potential that students have but don't know they have.
2. Orient them and help them understand their strengths and weaknesses.
3. Help students find their vocation, and I don't mean just an occupation, a job. I mean a calling to a particular course of action or occupation.
4. Transform the students by helping them find the knowledge and awareness they don't already have.

To reach these goals and best help our students, we must pursue understanding our students' psychological, emotional, and physical selves to the best of our abilities.

Psychological and Emotional Understanding

It starts with learning their names. Talk to them. Get to know them. Some students want to scream at you, some students don't even want you to look at them, and still others want to speak with you one-on-one like a friend. Some students are completely removed from the teacher. Who are they? Why are they there? Where do they come from? Whether a student is there to become a professional or to take a break from a job as a telemarketer, or is there because her mother or a family member is an ex-dancer, it is important to know who they are so that we can best assist/teach/educate/help them.

For me there's no difference between teaching an amateur and teaching a professional. Both receive the same care and deserve the same high level of education. I educate their minds and bodies, and I aim to lift their spirits! The quality of teaching is the same for both amateur and professional students. I will not avoid teaching a student how to turn out correctly just because they'll never become a professional ballet dancer. Regardless of who they are and their reasons for taking my class, they deserve attention and care in order to learn technique and fine-tune their proprioception, their body's ability to sense movement, action, and location.

Remember the dinner analogy I mentioned above?

A good class is like an amazing dinner full of proteins,
carbohydrates, fruit, veggies, and dairy products. But your students can't eat
the whole meal at once. Each student takes what they need, and
everyone needs different things at different moments of their life. But you
as a cook must always offer a nutritious meal to everyone.
Teaching is generosity without expectations!

Physical Understanding

In addition to understanding our students' psychological makeup, we must understand our students' physical condition. The physical component—understanding students' body structures—helps us guide students to an appropriate balance of strength and flexibility, both of which are necessary for a dancer to perform movements without injury.

Sometimes, a teacher can help a student produce a beautiful shape but does not understand the mechanism by which this shape came into existence. If a teacher was born with a versatile dancer's body that can naturally express the ballet vocabulary, and that teacher is responsible for training other people's bodies that are different from his, the teacher may have difficulty explaining how to achieve the shape because he has been producing many beautiful shapes naturally, intuitively. How do you solve this issue? How do you guide your students to navigate their own bodies? My answer: technique and a deep understanding of anatomy! As teachers, we need to adapt and give personal corrections to each student because each body and each learning process is different.

For some people it helps when I talk about the "alignment of their bones." Others respond to discussion of muscles and muscle tone, or the center of energy and energy projection. Others learn best by using visualization techniques. Still others rely on their imaginations. Some prefer anatomical facts and some use imagery out of their bodies, comparing a movement with a movement in nature. They can move "like a wave crashing on the beach," for example.

You might explain some movement or phrase from different angles and with a specific vocabulary, exploring the shape of the bones and how the joints articulate or align, or the mechanism by which a muscle contracts or releases, or how many types of contractions occur in the skeletal muscles to find the center of energy in the body and discover how it flows. The teacher must study a great deal to have at hand all these tools and elements to communicate as clearly and precisely as possible with their students.

When I teach, I move and walk around the classroom and give corrections to each individual student. Each correction is very specific because each student's physical movement is unique with regard to structure, constitution, psychology, cultural background, etc. It is the teacher's job to try to educate each student's body as precisely as we can.

One way I like to think about understanding bodily structures is through the concept of "tension"—the accumulation of energy in a certain part of the body. Sometimes we have an excess of tension because we don't know how to channel and project the energy in space. Why does this happen? Perhaps the primary muscles that execute an action are weak so the rest of the muscular system is in "emergency mode" and another muscle group is needed to assist. Doing a *développé en avant* (the leg at 90 degrees in front of the body) is difficult to execute if the emotions are stored in the muscle group needed to realize the action. Instead of releasing the energy to project the leg into space, the energy is accumulated in the muscle group, making it impossible to do the movement correctly.

You may want to do a big jump like a *grand jeté*, but you have tension in your neck, in your hands, or your arms; or you do not know how to jump from your center of energy; or you focus on your spine or hips as a center; or you've overworked certain parts of your body and have accumulated tension there. As a result, you cannot ascend and defy gravity because the legs are just the springs!

Sometimes the problem is identifying your center of energy, the motor of your movement, and sometimes you use superficial muscles that are overdeveloped but your innermost muscles are weak. Tension indicates that you are overusing your muscles. Why do a movement and use 100% of your energy when you can use just 20% and do it efficiently? A teacher can help you become more conscious of how to control your muscle tone.

How much tension does your student have in their body? Where does their body accumulate tension? If the teacher understands the student's body type, psychology, and prior training, she can help the student channel and release energy through liberation and projection.

If a dancer is extremely tense, their muscles are stiff and the movement range will be limited even when they think they're relaxed. It is important for a teacher to understand the students' body structures because you will support them differently according to their muscle tone. We have to distinguish tension versus muscle tone to target our training. A person who has strong muscle tone typically has problems with flexibility, and a person with soft muscle tone will have problems with strength. A performer who has developed well-balanced strength and flexibility moves most efficiently and healthily. Injuries are a product of the imbalance between flexibility and strength.

As teachers, we try to support students to attain a middle ground with an awareness of energy expenditure, what I call "economy of movement" or "efficient energy mode." I compare the use and release of energy to turning on a water faucet. When you open a faucet for the first time, you may open it too much and you get all wet. You then learn that you will get all wet if you open the faucet too far, so the second time you open it just a little, but you don't get enough water on your hands this way. The third time, you find the middle point and get just the right amount of water to wash your hands.

The same thing happens when we do a movement. We use too much energy in the beginning because we want to do it whether it is correct or not, I call this doing the movement "in emergency mode." With practice, we figure out just the right amount of energy to do the movement correctly. That is why we need repetition. Repetition in dance is important. **Repetition plus consciousness is the solution.**

Teachers also help students master the isolation and coordination aspect of their own technique. As a teacher you should challenge students to experience, study, and understand the concept of isolation in regard to the use of energy and muscles. Is the student able to isolate and activate different muscles in the legs independently and not think of or use their legs like a chorizo (sausage)? Understanding the function of the different muscle groups in their legs individually and in coordination will result in proper technique and muscle work and development. One example is to energetically connect the calcaneus (heel) bone to the greater trochanter at the top of the femur to protect and align the ankle, knee, and hip joints in a landing after a big jump!

Training a performer and a dancer takes years of delicate dedication, specificity, and conscientious work to help students achieve muscular isolation, fascia awareness, and energy coordination—all at once. As a teacher, you need to immediately identify students' problems with connectivity, isolation, and proprioception to help them face difficulties with biomechanics and use their bodies as instruments of their expression. To do this, a teacher must maintain a fluid, precise, and sincere dialogue, explaining the things that you observe and explaining what you know, as well as what you don't know but that you can help the student address.

Top: Anabella teaching "My Body, My Country" body mapping workshop at Queens Museum, NY, 2019
Bottom: Anabella teaching "My Body, My Country" body mapping workshop at Columbia University, NYC, 2019

Stimulus, Interest, Empowerment, Possibilities, and Human Sensibilities

In preparing a class, I feel it's important to keep five key class components in mind while remembering your goals for understanding your students. I describe these components in the next few paragraphs. They are as follows:

- Stimulate students
- Create interest
- Empower students
- Show students different possibilities
- Develop human sensibilities

Stimulate Students

A stimulus is an impulse that motivates a person to develop aesthetically, artistically, creatively, and socially. You need to make students like what they are doing and enjoy it. If they're not enjoying learning, it's your job to try other approaches and stimulate in different ways. Make them enthusiastic about the process of learning, the process of discovering themselves. The educational journey is a journey of self-realization and self-investment.

Create Interest

We must create interest in art, dance, and other arts. I remember one dance history student who was studying to become a dentist at the university where I taught. When he first arrived in my class, he didn't care about dance at all. He just took the class because it fit into his schedule and fulfilled a requirement. It was my job to create interest in dance and dance history for him. The homework for that class included going to see live shows and writing impressions of them. Even after he had done all of the homework, he kept going to the ballet. Why? He had a lot of dates. He loved to bring his dates to the performances and tell them about what he was learning in class. That's how I created an interest in dance for that particular student. Creating interest and curiosity is not an easy thing, but we must try! Encourage a hunger to learn and discover something new.

Empower Students

A teacher must discover what the students' strong and weak points are and empower them to take responsibility for their uniqueness. One student told me, "I really like your class, Anabella, because I do not feel that you compete with us." That was a very revealing comment for me. Why would I compete with my students? We do not build a top-down relationship with our students. To empower students, a teacher must highlight students' strengths and weaknesses, all with the goal of strengthening each student in the ways that they need. A large part of my job is to encourage, not to direct students in one direction or another. It is not our job to say, "You are not going to become a professional dancer," or "You are going to be a choreographer." I experienced those situations as a student. One teacher told me that I would never be a professional dancer. Some teachers might say, "She has the body to be a dancer," or "She doesn't have the body to be a dancer." What does that mean? Who are we to say what a student will or will not be? Our job is to strengthen the student's education and the student's power in everything—physiologically, psychologically, creatively, in every way. Empowering our students makes them aware of their strengths and weaknesses, their limits and their talents. Deep care is the answer.

Show Students Different Possibilities

As teachers, it is also our responsibility to consider the perspective that students have of themselves and the field of dance. One of my dance students wanted to be a company member of American Ballet Theater (ABT). I knew that wouldn't happen: He had started to study ballet when he was 15 years old, which is considered late for ABT. Since he wasn't ready to accept that, it was my job to show him other possibilities in the field of dance outside ABT, outside having a career as a professional ballet dancer, so that when he was ready, he would have the tools he needed to make sensible, realistic choices for his career. I directed him to possibilities among modern and contemporary dance companies.

I grew up studying flamenco and ballet. I had two different perspectives about dance: one as a folk dance and the other a dance spectacle. Having both of these perspectives opened my eyes to opportunities in the field of dance that I may not have identified otherwise. The problem with life experience is that the career of a performer or a dancer is so short that by the time you have discovered yourself, you are 30 years old and your career may be nearly over.

It is a teacher's responsibility to show students the opportunities available to them in the dance field: You can choreograph, teach, write about dance and become a dance critic or dance historian, produce dance, be a dance notator, be a physical therapist or fitness trainer, and so on. That is why it is important that as a teacher you have a professional career as well because your students can look to you as an example of a possible dance career.

Develop Human Sensibilities

Sometimes it seems that dancers become a little inhuman. They want to become super-flexible, super-strong superheros, avoiding reality and human emotions. It's easy to forget that we're still human. I feel it's part of my job as a teacher to develop students as human beings just as much as I support their technical excellence. José Limón says "I believe that we are never more truly and profoundly human than when we dance." Dance is a way to enhance your generosity and compassion. Dance is a holistic way of living. As a dance teacher and mentor you must cultivate ethical values while helping students think for themselves.

I emphasize critical thinking and personal life experience as it relates to dance. Wherever I go, I teach with a human and comprehensive pedagogy in which creativity, ethics, and aesthetics are intertwined. I consider the practice of any art a meditation on life. I dedicate my life to investigating the interior logic of performance and the role of a dancer in our culture today.

Nothing fulfills me more than to discover different processes of creation, becoming, and transformation. My curious mind and heart always lead me to a fresh beginning, where creativity helps me to transcend ideas and rules, creating meaningful methods. I celebrate, respond, protest, scream, cry, and laugh about life through dance.

My daily meditation is observing the bodies of my dancers and students in fine detail and with love as their expressions (mental, emotional, and spiritual) emanate and emerge. They flourish in each rehearsal or class. It's like observing nature reveal itself in front of your eyes, like a plant growing from seed and becoming a tree with flowers and fruits.

My profession allows me to experience generosity, compassion, altruism, empathy, tolerance, patience, and gratitude. I value respect and love for others and receive it in return. I give myself totally to the learning process.

The art of teaching is about contemplation, appreciation, reflection, exchange, detailed observation, assimilation, and developing a deeper human consciousness.

I am humbled, grateful, and thankful for every student, dancer, artist, collaborator, institution, and organization that lets me share my point of view.

Top Left: Anabella teaching "My Body, My Country" body mapping workshop at Queens Museum, NY, 2019
Top Right: Anabella teaching at Peridance Center, NYC, 2017
Bottom: ALDD rehearsal at DMAC, NYC, 2016

CHAPTER 5.
UNDERSTANDING CONTEXT

As we need to understand our individual students, we must also understand the institutional and cultural contexts in which we operate. What is the mission statement of the institution that we serve? What is its vision? What are its goals? How does teaching at a professional dance school differ from teaching at a university? How different is teaching in a small town from teaching in a world capital? Who are the people who attend your classes? Just as we need to understand our educational goals and our students' individual goals, we need to understand the goals of the institution where we teach. If we give private lessons, our individual students become the institution with their own motives, hopes, expectations, and past experiences. We teachers, students, and institutions need to establish our expectations and goals according to these details and circumstances. To do that we must identify a specific pedagogy, methodology, and didactic. Please see the definitions of pedagogy and methodology on pages page 22-23.

I must understand the community in which I teach and consider its development, both socially and culturally, as well as its specific artistic values as I develop a sensible pedagogy, methodology, and didactics. In my 35 years as an educator in more than 50 institutions in three continents, only five institutions informed me of their values and goals via a handout they gave me or regular staff and faculty meetings. So, what is happening in our dance field? Do teachers understand there is a trade-off between the expectations of the institutions and one's own goals? I feel the answer is to cultivate the values of altruism, selflessness, and generosity among students, staff, and faculty. To serve people, art, and institutions well we must first do research and evaluate what has to be done, how, when, and why.

Cultural Context

What is the specific culture where you work? What is the cultural background of the institution and its individuals, such as students, staff and faculty? How do you establish a relationship between your own cultural background and that of the institution?

Throughout my career, I did not always teach the same subject or use the same methodologies in my in-person and online classes in ballet, point, modern, dance theater, dance composition/choreography, dance history, dance criticism, anatomy, Argentine tango, pedagogy and methodology of teaching dance, and even theater makeup! Different institutions, cities, and countries need different approaches.

I adapted and transformed my approaches according to where I taught at the time. In Rome, Italy, I taught modern dance for a renowned government-supported dance studio whose main focus was ballet. How I taught modern dance there was completely different from how I taught modern dance at New York City's Wagner College, where the main focus is on training musical theater dancers. The content of my classes was very similar, but they were different. How well known is American modern dance in Italy and how well known is it in New York City? What popular culture are the people of these different communities aware of?

Once when I was in the city of Bahia Blanca, Argentina, during one of my visits leading dance composition/choreography workshops, I had a big revelation: The Municipal Theater, which is supported by the city of Bahia Blanca and also partially by the Province State of Buenos Aires, was supposed to provide free space to dance companies and dance schools to perform and promote the art of dance, but they did not do so. They discriminate against the dance community and deny them theater space for shows and events. Instead, the Municipal Theater director at that time offered to my dance school, L'Atelier Centro Creativo de Danza, which my sister Pamela directed, a big basketball gym in which to perform. Keep in mind that the students performed ballet en point and wore shoes while performing flamenco! How were they to dance on a basketball floor? This space is not appropriate for this type of dance! Dance is not a sport!

In this case, as a teacher I needed to understand how Argentine society and the Municipal Theater as an institution undervalue and underestimate art and dance. For Argentina, sport is a big part of the culture, but art isn't as big. How am I to prepare and teach future generations of dancers and choreographers in a society like that? Many parents probably tell their children when they arrive at high school, "Don't waste your time on dance. It's best that you prepare to study to become a lawyer or a doctor when you arrive at the university." Knowing about Argentine society determines how I teach, how I speak to parents about the importance of art and dance, and how I explain, promote, and advocate for arts education.

A long time ago in New York City, I was giving private tango lessons to a professional modern dancer from Peru. We both spoke the same language: dance and Spanish. I was giving her a correction about the tango walk and I told her in Spanish with humor, "When you walk, please make your ankles touch each other in every step. Otherwise, even two dogs can pass between your legs!" In Argentina you would think a comment like that is super funny. My Peruvian student didn't, however. She took great offense, and that was with both of us speaking Spanish! You see? It's not only languages that can be different. It can be the culture, the background, the life experience. So how can we communicate, how can we be funny, polite, and respectful when you teach? Be careful, humor is a delicate thing!

It's interesting to experience different cultures as a teacher. Some societies applaud the teacher who is sweet and soft spoken, some appreciate the strict and authoritarian teacher. Some cultures approve of a teacher who screams at students and even sometimes uses foul language to get the best from students. In some cultures they respect the self-taught teacher or experienced dancer less, even though that might seem contradictory to the popular narrative. In some cultures having papers and certificates that validate your academic life are more important than professional experience!

In my native Argentina, I found that dance education strongly emphasized developing a critical point of view (though maybe this is because we are a very anarchical society). Argentines encourage individuals' self-discipline, self-motivated curiosity, and active engagement in search of artistic identity, perhaps because we don't have the economic resources to develop and create strong institutions that don't depend on government funding, with all its related budget cuts and strikes!

Top: "The Night That You Stopped Acting/La Noche Que Dejaste de Actuar" performance at West Park Presbyterian Church, NYC, 2022
Bottom Left: "No More Beautiful Dances" performance at Columbia University, NYC, 2019
Bottom Right: "A bone to pick with you" performance at Crossroads Festival at Judson Church, NYC, 2021

Institutional Context

I remember when I was teaching at a very highly regarded university, and that institution gave me a 50-page book about its institutional goals, policies, and vision culture that I was expected to read before I signed my contract. I didn't agree with some things, but I knew what I was expected to do and what the institutional values were. I respect this greatly! Sometimes you're faced with the opposite situation and you really don't know what a school or institution's objectives are. Sometimes not even the director or staff of the institution where you teach knows what the institution's objectives are. How will I succeed as an educator in that atmosphere?

Your job as a teacher is to ask about cultural and institutional expectations. I find myself in many meetings with institutions I work at asking questions about institutional expectations. Here are some questions I find helpful to ask:

1. What do you expect me to do here besides teaching dance to creative individuals?
2. Do you expect me to produce students with stronger technical awareness in dance?
3. Do you expect me to educate, teach, or just train your students?
4. Do you expect me to create an audience for dance among your students?
5. Do you expect me to guide the students to be better citizens of the world?
6. Do you want your students to cultivate a love of art in general?
7. What is the profile of an average student?
8. What is the profile of an average alumnus?

Sometimes institutions provide teachers with lots of information about their objectives, but sometimes it's up to the teacher to ask the institution about those things. You as a teacher and the institution where you work need to make all expectations clear from the beginning.

The better you understand the community you are teaching in, the better you can understand which tools you will use to successfully adapt to your students' needs, especially now that education is very globalized because of easy access to international information. This question of cultural and institutional context is one of the most important for us to understand as teachers.

Dance Trends Context

Today students have access to so many different dance techniques and styles and can study Butoh, folk dance, Graham, ballet, hip-hop, or contemporary in the same institution or online! They have access to an enormous repository of books and online platforms like Vimeo, YouTube, and podcasts via which they can view, study, or research dance online. This is an amazingly rich and confusing panorama of choices, especially for a beginner dancer who does not know what to choose from. How do we as teachers guide students to choose well? Are we giving them the tools to develop their own tastes?

We have one human body, one skeleton, and one muscular system. That has never changed. What makes techniques and styles different is the intention behind movements. Where you move from? What makes you dance? Dance is a point of view of life. Intention is what changes the technique, not the movement itself. With students having access to so many different techniques and styles when they are training, what has changed is that dancers are more able to realize commonalities across techniques around the world. They can start to find the parts of different techniques and styles that make sense for their own bodies, vocabularies, cultural backgrounds, nationalities, and ways they see life. As teachers we need to be by their side to guide them and provide a support system, to make them aware of their choices and what the "dance market" offers them.

We often favor the more the merrier, but this does not always work, especially in the formation of a dancer or performer. We need deep education, not shallow or superficial knowledge. Dance students need to master and deeply understand one or two techniques as they build their foundations. Once their foundation is solid, they can approach other techniques and styles with maturity.

In my teaching, I emphasize critical thinking and personal life experience as it relates to art, dance, and performance.

Warning: The democratization of information in social media, specifically learning and teaching dance, is not enough to create an artist or a performer. The new generation of dancers is bombarded with tons of information and they often feel lost. They have problems discerning levels of quality, and their vision is diluted. Having all the information in the world instantly at your fingertips does not make you smarter or truly knowledgeable in any subject.

Image Above: "The Night That You Stopped Acting/La Noche Que Dejaste de Actuar" performance at Estrogenius Festival, NYC, 2023

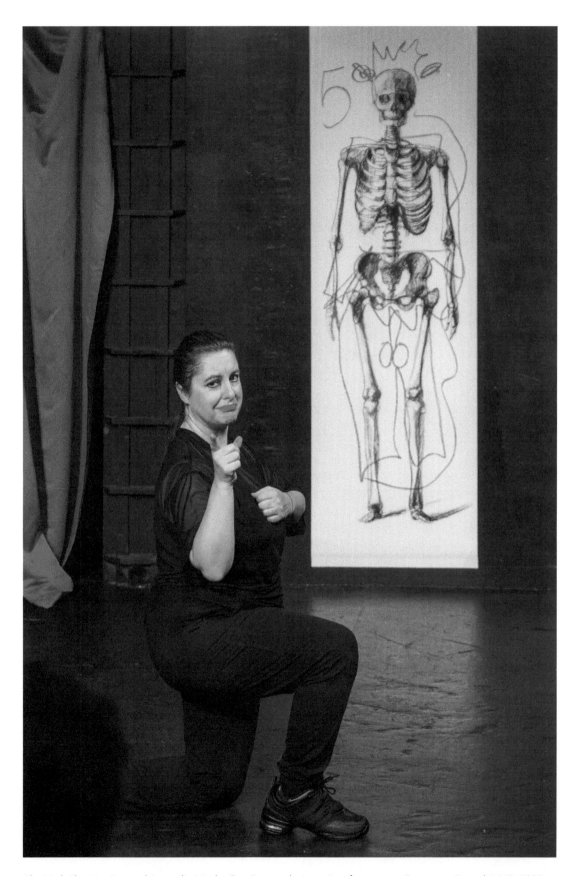

"The Night That You Stopped Acting/La Noche Que Dejaste de Actuar" performance at Estrogenius Festival, NYC, 2023

CHAPTER 6.
TEACHING ARTISTS VS. TECHNICIANS:
TECHNIQUE AND POINT OF VIEW

Distinction Between Artists and Technicians

This book is about teaching artists, technicians, and performers. For me being a dance artist and being a technically proficient dancer are two different things. Not every dancer or performer is an artist. To be an artist is much more than doing the "tricks" (like splits or five consecutive pirouettes) or performing on a stage.

Dance artists are athletes plus something extra. Is it possible to teach someone to become an artist? I think students are who they are. A teacher can give a student the tools to find their way to their own voice, whatever that might be, but I don't think someone can be taught to be an artist. I think you are either an artist or not. You have the hunger and thirst or not. I can inspire someone but only up to a certain point. It's like your personality. When you study you get the tools to understand yourself. You shape yourself, you find your way, your style, and your identity, and of course you learn a craft. When you study dance, you try different styles and techniques and then you pick a vocabulary of movement that suits your personality, your physicality, and your desires, that suits you emotionally and intellectually. You create your own vocabulary to express your own voice, your own point of view of life.

Being an artist requires much more than training. You need to develop a point of view about life. It means finding your originality and uniqueness. We are all unique as human beings. Art takes craft and the ability to be generous about who you are, the ability to offer yourself to the world and at the same time to create a better society and a different way of seeing life. "Artist" is not a synonym for "dancer." Artists inspire other people. Artists push the envelope, transgress, and shake the status quo.

Can a dancer who doesn't have very strong technique be an artist? Yes. Limitations in an artist are opportunities to be unique. Being a good technician does not push the boundaries of what art can be.

There are many examples, among them Jorge Donn (1947-1992), a renowned Argentine who danced for Maurice Béjart and Ballet XX Century. He was unique.

If you look at some of his videos, you can see that he doesn't have a "perfect" turnout or feet for a "standard" dancer, but he is certainly an artist. Technique doesn't look the same in different bodies. Technique is a way of controlling your body, your expression, and your emotions, and you can use different techniques to control them in different ways. When you go to a ballet performance, the dancers will be well trained in ballet technique in order to communicate the artistic vision of ballet choreography. Technique, or control of the body, gives an artist the ability to communicate. Artists don't always fit the box of an existing technique. In fact, many artists don't "fit" any place because new ideas are generally not fashionable. New ideas typically become fashionable only later.

Artists need to break the mold and depart from the standard way of doing things. You must challenge the way you and others see life by tapping your difference and your creativity. If you conform and only follow what has gone before, you may find that you're never able to find your own voice. Being an artist is hard. It takes a lot of courage to be different because nearly all of us want to belong. We want to be part of something. Working as an artist is very lonely.

How long does it take to find yourself in life and as an artist? It depends on how hungry you are, how lazy you are, how much you believe in yourself, whether you have a system that can support you, such as a family, financial assets, professional connections, and many other things. Sometimes people need a support system, but sometimes people prove stronger without support.

There's no school on how to become an artist! Life is the school.
You discover yourself in your own time. It also depends on culture and place.
Maybe you live in a place that emphasizes conforming to specific
social ideas, and it's much harder to be an individual.

Artists communicate something that they feel is urgent for them, for the world. Part of being a dance artist is honestly believing in the material as a performer and doing it as openly as possible. Performers and dance artists must believe in the powers of their movements and actions in order to be understood. The conviction must be total. Otherwise they won't convey their message. Dancers and choreographers put forth a question that they frame in metaphors, images, visions, sounds, and textures. The audience engages in that question when they watch the performance, and they then formulate their own opinion about it. It's an open two-way communication between artist and audience. *Metakinesis* is the communication between the performance and the audience. (Meta means empathy and kinesis means movement.) This is how movement becomes contagious.

When someone states that "politicians are terrible," they are not making art. They are just sharing their opinion. Art is a way of asking a question—"Are politicians terrible?" for example—that generates different insights and interpretations.

Sometimes as a choreographer, what I want to share doesn't come across to the audience because I didn't craft the piece well or because I intentionally don't want to be explicit so the audience can slowly discover their own meaning. Whatever you put on stage, you want something from the audience more than just applause and "Great job!" Putting something on stage is not just about recognition, status, approval, or being "famous." It's about how vital it is to share something with someone. That's the power of gestures, the power of the moving body. You can change the way people see life through gestures and performance. There is something profoundly emotional going on in the world, as we care so much about something that we are moved to share it with an audience. One friend told me that dance is not a religion, but for me it is a religion.

Interestingly, I feel that technique sometimes blocks the body's natural expressivity. We all move differently. Our goal as dancers ought to be to enhance this natural way of moving versus learning a code of movement that erases our individuality, our way of moving in the world.

When you see Mikhail Baryshnikov (known as Misha) dancing, for example, you see him, not ballet technique. You see Misha moving. You do not think about his nice passé. Yes, he is doing it, but he is using technique as a language to make poetry. Sometimes we feel that we have to repeat technique exactly the same as the next person, but in doing so we erase the personality of the performer's movement. Technique is like a mold that you have to fit into, but no one has the same body, DNA, or personality. Everybody is different. This does not mean we have different ballet techniques, but we do have different approaches.

Technique is a tool with which to arrive at self-knowledge. If the technique or style you are studying opens you up to another consciousness, the technique and its teacher are doing their jobs. Working to look like other dancers is not working on technique. It is copying. It is working on an aesthetic outside of yourself. If you are a performer working to fit into a mold, please stop! You are erasing yourself. Technique is a way to find yourself, not a destination. It is like deciding that you want to be a painter to paint like Picasso. It's impossible. There was one Picasso in the world, and there is only one you in the world. You are different from Picasso. You will paint differently from Picasso. As teachers, it is our job to encourage students to find themselves as individuals and their own voices as artists rather than trying to fit them into a mold.

When I was training and performing dance, I didn't understand the dance culture that felt so superficial. The "Me, me, me! Look at me!" dance culture needs to be calibrated. Many dancers may be like that, but many are not. It's not about the tricks that you can do, it's about commitment to expressing an idea through those tricks. I guess that's why I complain about dance competitions because they cultivate dance as only a sport rather than as athleticism with a goal of artistic expression. Sometimes competition can be helpful, but sometimes it's not. It depends on the person.

Art cannot be competitive against others. Art is generosity.
The competition is with myself to be a better person and better artist every
day, to evolve, to have an open heart, mind, body, and spirit.

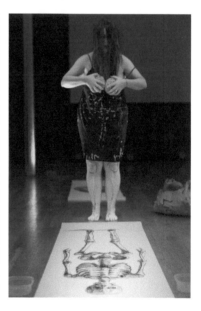

All Images: "Listen to Your Mother" performance at Movement Research at Judson Church, NYC, 2023

Implications for Teaching

Understanding the difference between artists and technicians means different things for teaching different types of classes and depends largely on your teaching goals. When I teach barre à terre, I focus much more on technique, whereas when I teach modern dance, I focus much more on artistry. Still, even in barre à terre, I tell my students to imagine that they are performing the vocabulary of movement they are using in class. But that's all secondary within the context of knowing fundamentals of bones, muscles, alignment, how energy moves through the body, how the breath works, etc. The next sections explore how we can apply ideas about teaching technicians and artists in practice.

"The Night That You Stopped Acting/La Noche Que Dejaste de Actuar" performance at BAAD, Bronx, 2023

CHAPTER 7.
TEACHING STRATEGIES

Teacher-Student Relationship

When students perceive that their teacher is still searching and working as an artist, I feel they become much more engaged in the material. At the performing arts universities, when faculty and teachers don't perform, create, or choreograph, don't keep their flames burning, I've noticed that students often relate to their teachers in a more removed way than when they study with people still engaged in their practice. I believe students benefit from seeing the creative process in action and their teachers sharing steps of the journey with them. As a teacher, you never stop learning. In fact, I'm convinced that a good teacher learns from her students. The student learns how to learn from watching you learn. The student learns from you as a human being, not just from the information you provide them.

I was 15 years old when I started teaching dance. I experimented a lot with my students. I felt that because I was so young and was a very good dancer, they trusted me implicitly, no matter what I did. They would say, "Oh, I want to be like you, Anabella!" So, they followed me, even if the class wasn't prepared that well. I think that what mattered was that I was transparent, naive. I gave myself entirely to my students, to my art. It didn't matter how young I was or if I was teaching things incorrectly. The problem becomes when you grow up and you're still teaching things incorrectly.

Sometimes, when a new generation of dancers arrives, they're a little arrogant. They're invested in creating the most amazing thing in the world. It's human nature. I remember when I came to the United States to study dance composition/choreography and modern dance. In Argentina I studied ballet, flamenco, tango, and modern jazz.

When I came to the United States, I sought out the oldest living modern dance teachers and choreographers. I wanted to learn modern dance first- or secondhand. Many of these teachers told me, "Anabella, you are too ambitious!" I think they saw what I considered eagerness to learn as ambition. It took me time to understand what that meant. I don't know if I have less ambition now. I don't think so, but I'm not sure. Maybe one day I will learn. But I see that, to an extent, ambition is important. However, it's also important to keep an open mind and understand the teacher in front of you as not just an educator but as a human being. The more I study dance, the more I learn about others and about myself.

Another thing that's important about the student-teacher relationship is the idea of competition. One student from a professional training program in New York City once said to me, "I know I can trust you because you don't establish a competition with us." Some teachers compete with their students. That is extremely unwise, and it is very selfish. Maybe it comes from jealousy because the teacher is not as young as their students. Maybe they didn't have as many opportunities as their students, who seem to have everything. When you are older, you make your own choices. Your generosity and openness should increase.

When I was choreographing a piece for a dance festival in Argentina, the teacher and director of the company I danced for came to see what I was preparing. She told me that she didn't like the piece and that if I were to perform the piece for the festival, I would be cut from her company. She was jealous of me and of my choreography. After that, I left the company and continued choreographing on my own.

Another thing to touch on with regard to the student-teacher relationship in dance is dance's relationship to touch. When I first arrived in NYC from Europe and was teaching an open intermediate ballet class at a big dance school in New York City, I touched a dancer's arms to correct her *port de bras* (movement or placement of the arms). When, in reaction, she shouted, "Don't touch me!" I was surprised and frightened. I didn't understand how I could be a dance teacher and not touch the body of a student. If I couldn't touch a student's body, I couldn't give adequate feedback. I essentially couldn't teach them. I could not make them aware of their muscle work or tone, or the weight of their limbs. We are tangible bodies moving in space. We need touch to realize our materiality.

After the student shouted, we kept going with the class at the barre. But after we finished the barre and before we moved to the center, I told the student, "If you don't want anybody to touch you, and you can't accept corrections, you must study dance at home. Dance is about contact, about relationships and communication. It's about being part of the community. You have a relationship with the teacher, with the other dancers, and with the musician." The student left.

Dancers cannot be afraid of their own bodies. This question of touch is important, and you may encounter it in different ways, depending on where you teach and what kind of dance you teach. Each body is a world, and each body carries so much trauma.

Ask permission before you touch your students and have an open dialogue about fear and trauma. Healthy bodies in healthier minds.

Choreographer-Dancer Relationship

Sometimes the role of the choreographer can be mistaken for the role of a teacher, though there are many similarities. However, I aspire to think in a different way for my dance company. I hope to engage with my dancers not as students but, rather, as collaborators. They are equal in their artistic excellence and bring just as much as I do to the choreographic process and result. I personally can't work with a dancer who is not an artist. Sometimes the choreographer doesn't know exactly what she wants. She may have an intuition and want to work as a team with the dancers to sort things out.

Left: Anabella teaching online, NYC, 2020
Right: Anabella teaching at Heifetz Institute, VA, 2023

Teaching the Unmotivated Student

I'm sure any teacher reading this has had students who don't want to learn, don't want to work or improve. When that happens, I just let them be, but I don't ignore them. Your students trust you, and you must trust them. Maybe they don't want to take your class. Maybe they aren't interested in what you have to offer them. But we must assume that they still want to become a dancer, so we must trust their decision not to become deeply involved in your class material. You are trying to be there for whatever it is they need of you. Maybe they won't listen to your corrections, but then again maybe one day they'll be injured and they remember something you taught them. Or maybe one day something simply something clicks for them personally. As teachers we must trust and have hope. If I don't have hope or if I give up on my students, I'd best stop teaching. It's my job to hope. As I keep saying, teaching is generosity We can't teach if we are not generous.

Teaching Self-Discipline

What is self-discipline? The dictionary definition cites "self-discipline, correction or regulation of oneself for the sake of improvement." Synonyms include continence, restraint, self-command, self-containment, self-control, self-government, self-mastery, self-possession, self-restraint, will, and willpower.

For me, self-discipline is the key to working on the flexibility and strength of one's mind, body, and spirit. Without self-discipline, the life of an artist is impossible.

Self-discipline includes respect for what you love. It is your ability to continue working on your art despite being tired one day or sick another, or being faced with any number of challenges that arise.

No one is going to scream at you and tell you what to do and when to do it. You must not count on having someone other than yourself telling you what to do.

As an artist, sometimes you struggle to explain why you do the work. When you can't find a satisfying answer, self-discipline is there to rescue you.

You are responsible for yourself. We as dance teachers need to sow the seed of self-discipline in our students because at the end of the day, they will be alone with themselves making art. It's the same thing that a mother does with her child: She wants her child to be as independent and as self-sufficient as possible. That is also the role of a dance teacher.

Sometimes teachers (like mothers) are so possessive that to keep their students by their sides, they create a debilitating dependency. If dancers cannot be by themselves without the teacher's guidance, the students will fail drastically. Sometimes the bond between student and teacher turns out to be a negative restraint. Sometimes it intentionally or unintentionally springs from the rush of power that comes from controlling your students' creative lives.

A student might be with you for months or years before moving on. It's our job to know when to say, "Call me when you perform. Keep me updated about your life and career!" and then let them go.

"Listen to Your Mother" performance at La Mama Moves Festival, NYC, 2024

Self-discipline is a big word that we often don't take the time to digest, but in the end, for our students, it may be the most important concept.

As a dance artist, you are alone with yourself. You are connected to yourself. You assume responsibility and complete ownership of your mission as an artist. Below is a list of a few words that may help us begin to identify the many implications and facets of self-discipline:

- Self-taught
- Self-knowledge/Self-understanding
- Self-esteem
- Self-love
- Self-awareness
- Self-care

I love the word "self" because it empowers you as an artist, and at the same time it gives you a lot of responsibility. Many dancers have come to me and said that they had a "bad" teacher for five years. Perhaps that's true, but thanks to self-discipline, the dancer can choose to leave or move on. (Note: The term "bad' is relative! What could this mean? A teacher with insufficient or outdated knowledge? Bad intentions?)

Self-discipline empowers you, provides you with security and reassurance.

During my dance classes, beyond providing knowledge and information, it is very important—and sometimes difficult—for me to encourage my students to cultivate their self-esteem.

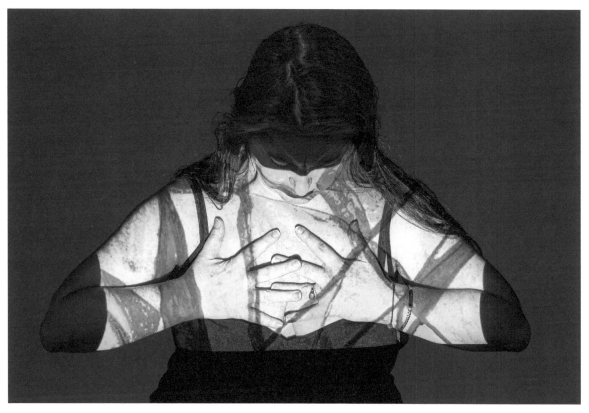

"Listen to Your Mother" performance at La Mama Moves Festival, NYC, 2024

If you see a student who does not understand something physically, but they understand it mentally, you must encourage them. Let them know that they are on the right path and will find their way. I usually say something to the effect of "I have patience and hope for you. You also need to have patience and empathy for yourself! When a child starts to walk, their parents need to encourage and stimulate them. Teachers must do the same for their students.

As a teacher, always have hope, patience, and trust in the development of your students. If a teacher loses hope and stops correcting students or stops saying "You're doing great!"—and I unfortunately see this a lot—the students lose their hope and self-esteem.

If you are a dance teacher and you've lost hope, you cannot teach because you do not trust your students' ability to improve. The students need your full commitment. Otherwise they can never build their sense of security and self-esteem necessary for self-discipline.

For me, hope comes naturally most of the time, though sometimes I need to force it because not all dancers will be professionals, but they can still be dance enthusiasts, dance advocates, members of the dance audience, etc.

That is hope.

You must believe that through dance education you can change people's lives! You can make an impact on the world by changing someone's feelings about themselves!

Self-Awareness

Regardless of whether you're teaching a performer, artist or dance technician, at least one fundamental component remains the same: training of students' self-knowledge, of knowing who they are.

When we come to dance class, we often do not recognize ourselves and our own potential. We typically do not accept who we are with all of our qualities and imperfections. Your physical technical training must work together with your self-awareness. Your body is not just a container. It is you. There is no division between the mind, the body, and the spirit. We are all of this at once!

It is you moving on stage. You are exposing your physical, psychological, and spiritual self. Your training must incorporate your humanity.

I have found that performers or dancers—even professional dancers—who have been training for eight or nine years have often forgotten that they are human beings. This means that as performers they struggle because their psychological and spiritual selves aren't integrated with their physically trained selves. This is problematic because the purpose of performance is to communicate with an audience. If an audience can't identify with the human components of what they see in performance, the audience may be initially impressed with a dancer's supernatural physical movements, but after a while all these tricks become boring. We are the mirrors of our audiences.

It is when an audience finds a psychological and spiritual connection with the dancers on stage that the communication starts to happen. Knowing a few physical tricks is helpful, but the goal behind doing them is not just to demonstrate them. It's to communicate something. The performer is the medium, not the end— the messenger, not the message.

"Listen to Your Mother" performance at La Mama Moves Festival, NYC, 2024

Another way to think about self-awareness is to think about stage presence, which I always talk about.

It is about knowing why you dedicate your life to performance. It is about knowing who you are and what your role as messenger is. It is about having technique and a system of consciousness that is distinct from that of regular life.

You study your body to be an instrument of communication. That study involves learning how to be in your body and how to be in space. We need to learn technique as performers and dancers. Whatever technique it is, it is integral to being a performer or dancer to have a system with which to control your body, your mind, and your emotions and learn to be conscious of how your movement expresses forms, ideas, or emotions.

"Listen to Your Mother" performance at La Mama Moves Festival, NYC, 2024

Acquiring consciousness, proprioception, and self-awareness through technique requires focus, concentration, sensibility, love, and time. When I teach barre à terre, for example, some students think they will understand ideas about such movements as en dehors (the turned out rotation of the legs) in an hour and a half, whereas it takes six months to a year for the body to acquire that kind of physical, intellectual, and psychological knowledge—if you're lucky, if you attend class regularly, and you practice outside of class. Dreams take hard work, consistency, and responsibility. When you begin performing, you develop an additional responsibility for the idea you are communicating. What are you saying? How are you saying it? How do you communicate with the audience? Why?

Progressing from the initial stages of learning technique through to performance takes an immense amount of care, love, trust, patience, and investment.

> *Technique also serves to open yourself to flexibility in the way that your mind, body, and spirit engage. Technique helps you to transform.*

Ironically, technique helps us to become more human because as performers on stage, our job is to communicate and magnify ideas about the human experience. Otherwise you look like a puppet, like a robot. Techniques that focus only on control of the body and not the mind and spirit can sometimes create physical monsters instead of performers who are open and are able to achieve an emotional reflection about life.

How does this all come back to teaching? As teachers, when we teach material, it's important to think about not just preparing for a class but also about our students as future dancers, teachers, choreographers, or just audience members who pass along the knowledge we give them to future generations. We must be prepared to transfer to them knowledge about the entirety of what technique is: critical eyes, consciousness, open heart, and responsibility for everything they do.

External Images: Use of Video for Study

There are, of course, challenges to teaching self-awareness, especially when it comes to the use of videos in training. It can sometimes be counterproductive for dancers to see themselves on video during the creative process or rehearsal. They may start to see themselves from the outside in highly critical terms. Their self-trust can be eroded, and they tear themselves apart, usually because of insecurities regarding their physical structure and appearance.

It takes practice to know how to look at yourself on video as a performer or a dancer. You must learn what to look for. Are you analyzing your use of the physical space? Your projection of energy? Changes in dynamics, etc.?

If we're not practiced in watching ourselves on video, we often develop skewed ideas about what we actually look like ("I look fat/short/tall/skinny"). But that's not the point of watching yourself, and it's also not what dancing is about. You must learn to view class, rehearsal, or performance videos just to see what you are doing and whether you can openly express an idea to the audience.

It's important to learn how to see yourself without personal attachment. Few people can do that, but you can get better at doing so with practice. It's also important to keep in mind when watching yourself that emotional expression on camera is totally different from live performance. The camera misses a lot of information from 3D to 2D. That's why dance film is its own art form. I believe this should be a core part of contemporary training methodologies because watching ourselves on video is now such an integral part of creative and rehearsal processes.

I am convinced that when you start training in any technique or style as an artist or technician, it is crucial for you to proactively develop muscle memory. Many teachers have students perform the same movements or exercises over and over again, resulting in the students learning to repeat shapes and phrases like parrots. Students then develop a type of external emergency response so the movement is disconnected from an internal awareness of how and why a movement is performed. In this way, the student learns to approach movement externally—from the outside. Let's imagine, for example, a teacher asking one of the students to hold his right leg à la seconde at 120 degrees for 45 seconds. The student will try to do it, but he won't understand what muscles to use and how to execute a movement and the complexities of the biomechanics. He will copy the movement with the grace and intelligence of a zombie. Remember that energy, consciousness, and intention create the shapes and not vice versa! As a result, dancers are often disconnected from the physical, emotional, and spiritual aspects of dance and technique.

We teachers don't want to train parrots. We aim to teach!
We want students to understand and find the motivation for different
movements and muscular usage from an internal necessity.

Sometimes in workshops, I make students draw a physical map of how they perceive themselves—a form of body mapping. The drawing describes how they energetically, emotionally, and spiritually see themselves. This exercise is based on different workshops that I took about drawing and on a book published by an institute in Buenos Aires called Instituto de la Máscara (The Mask Institute). The first time I did this exercise it was fantastic. I found that I could identify the tense parts of my body, where I was soft, where I felt that movement was blocked, where energy was, whether I felt energy flow more in my arms or my legs or the top of my head. This is an interesting exercise because it is like a game.

Top: "Listen to Your Mother" performance at La Mama Moves Festival, NYC, 2024
Bottom: "Listen to Your Mother" performance at La Mama Moves Festival, NYC, 2024

Drawing different types of exercises and answering a different set of questions, you realize how much you know and how much you don't know about your body.

Since 2018, I have been teaching my "My Body, My Country" body mapping exercise in museums and in dance theater classes in universities and cultural centers open to all communities. During these workshops, we ask many questions: How does our body become our homeland? What does it mean to be a female human? How do our bodies become a receptacle and messenger of the multiple realities we are immersed in?

During the 90-minute workshop, participants use movements, words, and drawings to share their stories. Drawing their bodies on large rolls of paper, they explore how their bodies become receptacles and messengers of the multiple realities we are immersed in. The workshop challenges participants to think about how they view their stories in relation to themselves and their bodies. Body maps are a way of storytelling, much like totems that contain symbols with different meanings. Body maps allow us to connect with our memories and emotions to give voice and visibility to one's identity. (See Body Mapping image on page 33.)

There is a powerful relationship between the physical and spiritual planes. The more we practice opening the door to that connection, the more consciousness we develop in the body, and the more the body can respond muscularly, organically, physically, and biomechanically, which in turn gives us more access to our emotional plane. Each movement that we do physically has some spiritual repercussions. We cannot ignore that dance is mind, body, and spirit.

Imagination, Innovation, and Creativity

Imagination, innovation, and creativity are all specific and important parts of training a dance artist. Sometimes we feel we need to train students' bodies or memories how to quickly pick up movement combinations, how to remember choreography, how to become stronger, or how to become more flexible. We often forget about educating a performer or a dancer about creativity, innovation, and imagination. Too often, dance training largely ignores these aspects of performance that are vital to becoming an artist. As teachers we therefore need to fill the gap between the training of a dancer and the training of a performer or actor. The ability to imagine, create, and innovate plays a tremendous role in dance training.

Imagination is the first step in making something that doesn't exist a reality.

The next step is innovation, and the third, creativity. As performers, this is what we do. Through our performance, we craft an emotional and physical space that didn't exist before. To perform, we need to have an imagination. I'll use Charlie Chaplin as an example. With a simple movement he can turn a mundane prop into something magical. This skill makes the audience transcend to another reality. Even a mundane prop can be transformed into something amazing.

Through dance, if we have imagination, as with just a small movement of a hand we're able to describe the simplicity of life and profundity of life at the same time. A small prop like a suitcase can be transformed into a book or a home. If you are unable to dream, to imagine, to envision something else, you end up with something that is completely practical, and art is not practical.

As kids we're all good at imagining things. As adults, it's something we must practice and must be part of our practices and training. That's why I always include improvisation in my classes. Improvising helps us practice imagination, opening the door to creativity. In my dance company, Anabella Lenzu/DanceDrama, we explore, reveal, and examine emotional histories, and the creative process is the magnifying glass. We distill the pure essence of real experience, real feelings, and real people. We stimulate and encourage audiences to identify with the characters on stage and undergo a catharsis of their own impulses and desires, removing the fourth wall that separates artist from audience. The search for the essential drama is transparent, so the audience is wholly involved in the transformative process. Both the dancers and the audience fuse in a psychological and emotional experience.

Dancers who lack the creativity or imagination to create characters and situations cannot help me as a choreographer, and I can't do their job for them. They need imaginations to create characters that are outside of themselves.

Innovation is the second step in making something that doesn't exist come to life. It comes in part from understanding history and tradition. Without understanding history and tradition—what came before—how can you be sure you're creating something new? As educators and teachers then, we must also prepare future artists with knowledge of history and tradition so they have the tools to innovate.

The third ability an artist must have is creativity. Part of creativity is having access to your life experiences and emotions to craft them into new solutions to a problem. Performers and dancers spend a lot of time in studios practicing and rehearsing. This often means that they don't have a lot of time to research, read, or study academically. At the same time, most performers are highly intellectual and experience life very intensely and critically. They are intellectuals of the body and of moving art. Their knowledge fuels creativity. Creativity survives within us every day. It is present in the way we dress, how we cook, and in our larger life choices. It seems to me that some people are born creative and some people learn to be creative.

Improvisation helps us teach skills that are stepping stones to imagination, innovation, and creativity. Improvisation makes the intangible tangible. Sometimes students are uncomfortable with improvising. It has a lot to do with the concept of play, which we tend to forget about as we get older. In giving a student feedback, I told her that I felt she was too serious to improvise, by which I meant that to improvise you must play with a concept and think beyond the specifics of the exercise's directives. Imagination and play go hand in hand. If you don't enjoy yourself, there is no experimentation, and your choices and results are narrow and dry.

Playing is hard for some students. When we begin training, we tend to be very serious in dance class or rehearsal, and we become afraid of being ridiculous with our bodies. We fear looking bad or silly, or not looking beautiful. We are working so hard on looking good that we do not know how to look ugly. We forget how to be goofy. We forget how to be horrible. We don't know how to make an obscene gesture. Too often much training cancels out many of the possibilities that ought to be available to us as performers. I sense a great deal of resistance from dancers when we do work that is not pretty, that is more ritually connected, that is more sexually connected, or that is on the edge. But as performers, our bodies need to be transformed. If we are afraid to envision these different emotions or to appear ugly, we self-censor our creativity and imagination, and we cannot be innovative.

This fear in dance training is different from what an actor feels in training. Actors learn to throw themselves, improvise, and use their imaginations. Their intuition and creativity guide them. They are trained into openness. In contrast, a dancer might think, "How will I look? Look at my butt! And I'm in tights!" This can block expression through the body. I do not find this limitation with actors. Training is supposed to help you achieve different states and explore different performance modes, but it can numb you in some ways or it can be an impediment. Did your teachers make you learn not to be ugly when you dance? One of my dance assistants always wanted to look pretty when she started dancing with me. We eventually hit a wall, and she actually changed so we could continue working together. What you do and how you express it is more important than how you look. How you look comes later. I feel that is a distinction between dance and theater.

Not all dancers are open to experimentation. Experimentation for dancers is often considered superficial. They experiment within the confines of a technique. I found that as a dancer, my contact with other performance methods opened me up a great deal. I had to look outside of the dance techniques I was taught to find a way to open myself up. I was trained in classical ballet, in a static way. Taking workshops in Butoh, masks, performance art, painting, sculpture, and film opened me up to other worlds.

When I saw Butoh dancers rolling their eyes and making vomiting movements with their tongues hanging out, it interested me enormously. It moved me. It was so powerful! I could see that the performers were freed from conventions, and when I began practicing Butoh myself, I was freed from judgments of myself and of others according to how pretty we looked. Distinctions between pretty art and ugly art, high art and low art, art or shit are all useless.

Top Left: Fiamma Lenzu-Carroll & Anabella rehearsing at La Mama Great Jones Studios, NYC, 2024

Bottom Left: Fiamma Lenzu-Carroll & Anabella performing at Salvatore LaRussa Outdoor Festival, Queens, NY, 2024

Right: Fiamma Lenzu-Carroll & Anabella during filming of "Becoming" at The Dragon's Egg residency, CT, 2022

Improvisation is a way to address these questions and insecurities. As teachers, we can guide our students by incorporating improvisation into our classes. There are many ways to incorporate improvisation into your technique class. A few simple examples follow.

- Allow the student to do a choreographed phrase of movement and then have them improvise—for, say, 32 counts—based on the theme of the choreographed phrase they performed.
- Teach a phrase of movement without explaining what it is about. Ask the student to fill this gap of themes and meaning so it is then up to the student to imagine the emotion, energy, and intent of the choreographic phrase.
- After students finish an improvisation or performing a phrase of movement that I've taught, I ask the dancers how they feel, what they imagine, or what images these movements evoke. Sometimes these images or what they imagine come from the senses; sometimes they're about narrative; and sometimes they're just about their own life experiences.

Now for the artistic application of improvisation. A student might be thinking, "Great! I can imagine something, but how am I going to apply it?"

I remember one solo choreographed by the great Maurice Béjart for the dancer Jorge Donn. It was called *Adagietto*. The dancer had one chair and a rose on the stage with him. Alone on a black stage with a white spotlight, Donn transformed the space with imagination. Sometimes what the dancer imagines is not the same as what the audience imagines, but we still believe the dancer's imagery. This Béjart masterpiece, which you can view on YouTube, is an example of creativity, imagination, and mastering the art of the solo.

Many times when I choreograph or perform a certain piece, I have images of cartoons doing funny things or physically impossible things running through my head. For example, I imagine a cartoon body stretching and becoming a giant like Alice from Alice in Wonderland. Sometimes I do a piece that is dramatic, but I imagine a weird and funny character from a cartoon. It helps me to achieve the dynamic or the shape or the sensation that I want, especially when I do choreography that requires a lot of changes in dynamics (the amount of energy used to perform a movement). So my imagination goes from something that is very serious and very dark to something that is very funny to help me achieve my goals as a performer. In *Black Swan*, the movie directed by Darren Aronofsky, we are made to wonder what is real life and what is a dream. We can use imagination to achieve different performance dynamics and flavors.

Sometimes I feel that movement evokes imagination. I remember studying and performing *Ballade* by Anna Sokolow. As a soloist, I was doing a big rond de jambe in the downstage right corner of the stage, with my hands open and parallel to the rond de jambe. In that movement I felt something I'd never felt before. I crossed time and space all the way from the United States to Argentina. It was so vivid. Even though I knew that the piece was not about that moment, I felt such a sensation of longing to do that big ronde de jambe!

I think the key is to be internally connected to yourself so when you learn a phrase of choreographed movement or improvise, you are very connected to yourself, thinking about how it affects you and how you feel you will affect the movement as well.

Sometimes when I'm working with my company, I know that my dancers are imagining things for a particular movement, so I stop them and ask what they are thinking about. In some cases, whatever they're imagining actually works, so I urge them to keep using their imagination because it is working. If it doesn't work, I ask them to imagine something else.

Without imagination there is no such thing as art, perhaps especially for dance when we sometimes lack scenography, music, costumes, or maybe even space or light. Sometimes we and/or the stage are bare. So with nothing except you and your movements, it is this imagination that enriches the work. Without imagination the movement is nothing. If you perform in Times Square without imagination people will not stop to watch!

Adaptability

When I came to the United States and I discovered American modern dance, I realized that I was a very good ballet dancer but I wasn't good at modern dance. I couldn't understand the principles until I really studied them, until I read about the different techniques and points of view. After deeply studying those principles, I became a versatile dancer. Now I can adapt. It's like speaking different languages. Sometimes I speak in English. Sometimes I speak in Spanish. Sometimes I speak in Italian or French. I am able to change dance techniques and performance methods according to what a choreographer asks of me. But in the beginning I couldn't adapt. I wasn't versatile enough or able to change.

I think adaptation is one of the most important skills for a performer or a dancer. You adapt to reflect a choreography project's goals, a dance company's style, a school's approach, or a director's point of view. You learn to be flexible not just with your body but also with your mind and heart. Every day we feel different, we react differently, but through technique we practice certain skills. We need to adapt to our internal and external circumstances: weather, humidity, your energy level, your health, an injury, any number of things. Being able to adapt and change allows you to transform yourself as a performer. I think any technique should prepare you for this transformation.

Coordination and Isolation

When you train as a performer or dancer you need to work on both coordination and isolation of movement. We need both skills to achieve clarity of intention when we move. We need to know what we are doing and what effect we want to have on the audience, even if the audience's reaction differs from what we expect. We must be very clear and very specific about our intention to communicate clearly with our audiences. This is what coordination and isolation help us achieve.

In both coordination and isolation we need to understand how impulses from the mind travel through the body. This takes patience because sometimes your mind understands this concept but your body does not, or the other way around. Sometimes it just takes a little more time for both to arrive on the same page. It's like a teabag: When you put it in hot water, it takes time for the water to turn to tea. Maybe you are a very intellectual dancer and you understand information right away, but it takes time for your body to understand that information.

When you study tap or flamenco and you want to do a shuffle or a tica (flamenco footwork step), you decide you want to make one sound but instead your body makes two or three. Why is the body moving ahead of what you think your mind is ordering? That is why it takes many years of training to have a thorough enough impact for your body to coordinate and communicate freely with your mind. Teachers may also need to be a little more patient with their students in this regard. Maybe a student needs six or nine more months to make the mind-body connection. It seems that the older we dancers get, the less patience we have. When we are young, development of the physical and intellectual happens at the same time, so it is typically easier to learn when we're younger. You may have been working on an idea for two years and someone else for five years, but the results can be the same.

Coordination and isolation are important skills to cultivate to be able to feel the body working as one unit, even if different parts of the body are doing different movements. Some techniques require complete isolation of one part of the body, but all parts of the body are important. As teachers we need to mix exercises and phrases of various types of movement in technique classes. This helps to ensure that we are developing passage of our students' impulses from their nervous systems to their minds and bodies.

When I speak about coordination and isolation, I am referring to body parts and about what takes place between the mind and the body, between intention and execution. In his book *Modern Dance Terminology*, Paul Love quotes José Limón as saying the following about isolation being intense concentration upon isolated parts of the body:

> Movement of the whole body is kept constantly in mind, but stress is also laid upon each of the parts. This may be achieved through an exercise specifically directed toward that part, or through an exercise of larger dimensions where now one and now another part become the focal point. The purpose is to increase awareness of the possibilities and potentialities of each part of the body and to sharpen and strengthen the movement.

ALDD's Performance "Pachamama: Mother World" at Sheen Center, NYC, 2016

Teaching Breath, Voice, and Muscular Drama

Breath and Voice

As I say in my classes, **"Breath is the gasoline of your muscles!"**

Breath is about life. A performer who doesn't breathe looks like a lifeless puppet!

And "The voice is a part of our body!"

I invite you, dancers and teachers, to explore the use of breath, to understand what is "muscular drama," and to appreciate how the voice influences movement and how movement influences the voice.

Janis Brenner, a renowned teacher and choreographer who lives in New York City, works a lot on understanding sounds that are created by movement. She trained in both dance and singing and performed with Meredith Monk and Alwin Nikolais. Her dance technique class helped me understand how to project my voice and how doing so influenced doing a swing or a triplet. The voice was an externalization of the dynamic of the movement. She asked us how we were breathing, whether we were breathing with the movement? Were we breathing before, during, or after the movement? Breath training is essential for any type of performer. Classes that focus on and explore breath rhythm are essential in a performer's training!

Scientifically speaking, oxygen allows cells to release energy needed for muscular work in dancing. We communicate with the audience through "muscular drama"—muscles contracted and released. The audience reads the tone of our muscles that liberate energy in space.

Inhaling through the nose does help filter the air, and exhaling through the nose helps control the amount of carbon dioxide leaving the body. But in dance our breath is like the gears of a car: We breathe according to the type of performance we are doing. How does the breath of a performer who is singing and dancing in musical theater differ from that of a ballet dancer who doesn't use her voice? How does an actor's breath differ from a dancer's? Many methods and techniques address these questions. Most dancers are not clear about how to breathe while they are dancing. So let us examine "breath rhythm," which is common to all kinds of performers and dancers.

All Images: ALDD's Performance "Pachamama: Mother World" at Sheen Center, NYC, 2016

Breath is used hand in hand with the projection of energy by a dancer and with voice projection by a singer or actor.

Breath rhythm has been defined and discussed by several well-known people in the worlds of dance and theater. In his book *Modern Dance Terminology*, Paul Love states that breath rhythm is "one of the natural physical rhythms which was observed and consciously used by followers of Isadora Duncan and others. The use of these natural rhythms was later formulated under the term 'dynamism.' The inhalation and expiration of breath, taken as a synthesis, provide natural physical rhythm and may be used as a dynamic governing principle, the various lengths and exaggerations providing a dynamic rhythm."

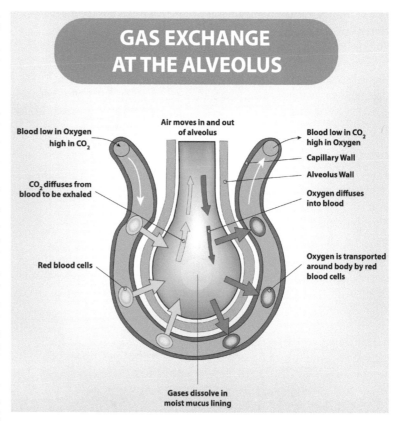

Constitution of muscle fibers

Breath rhythm also underlines Martha Graham's "contraction-release" principle and Doris Humphrey's "fall and recovery." Humphrey also remarked: " The breath rhythm in the time sense is a two-part phrase, the first longer than the second. In the space sense, it is a continuous movement of growing tension, followed by a letting go of tension, which finishes with an accent."

Emile Jacques-Dalcroze stated that "The trunk being the heaviest limb of the body, and that first influenced by emotion, owing to the action of the diaphragm, it follows that the most important and common instigator of all movements is the breathing. Breathing is at the basis of every manifestation of life, and plays as well aesthetically and physiologically, a role of the very highest importance in moving plastic."

How you breathe when performing depends a great deal on the type of dance you perform or technique you use. Some use just the maximum or median lung capacity, some use full breath capacity; some techniques require breathing through the nose or just the mouth. Others require inhaling and exhaling simultaneously from nose and mouth, or inhaling with your nose and exhaling with your mouth or vice versa!

When you breathe for theater, your breathing method typically depends on the voice projection demanded by the performance or the director. You may send air more deeply into your lungs, causing your abdominals to expand and dilate even more than in dance, or a director might ask you to inhale and exhale slowly to slow the delivery of your lines.

What happens when we dance and don't use our voices? In dance our lower abdominals and core muscles are on alert to gain total control of our movements, depending on the choreographic project that they are serving.

Breath and balance are hand in hand. When we exhale we feel more in control of our core due to our muscular control, and when we inhale we feel lighter than a balloon and have less control over our core muscles. Of course, our core muscles protect the spine and connect and establish relationships among the spine, head, ribs, and hips.

I wonder why we don't try to teach breath the same way in dance class so that we can explore how breath travels in our bodies. I'm fascinated by how we change the use of breath in choreography when we use text versus when we do not use it.

Muscular Drama

The liberation and projection of energy are intimately connected with the concept of "muscular drama," but what is it? How do we read dance as viewers? We do it with our bodies, and understanding the concept of muscular drama is one of the keys. Muscular drama has been a key concern for many theater and dance authorities over the years.

In *Acciones Corporales Dinámicas Metodología del Movimiento físico para Intérpretes Escénicos Inspirada en el Principio de Alteración del Equilibrio*, Sergio Sierra notes that the theatrical master Stanislavski observed that "While tension exists, one cannot speak of subtle, correct sensations, nor of a normal spiritual life of the character. Therefore, before starting creation, the muscles must be put in order so that they do not paralyze freedom of action."

Stanislavski highlights how muscle flaccidity, poor posture, or incorrect breathing can interfere with the plasticity of movement and the appearance of superfluous muscle tension results from poor use of the body. The inadequate use of the physical instrument is evident in actors given their exposure to the audience, and their work reveals how energy blockages that manifest themselves in unnecessary muscle tensions attack various segments of the body and reduce plasticity, coherence, and vitality from the movements created by the actor. In these cases internal motivations do not correspond to the external results, and there is no communion between what the actor feels and tries to do with what their body is really creating.

SKELETAL MUSCLE

Jerzy Grotowski observed that the use of the concepts of muscle tension and relaxation had been misinterpreted by many followers of Stanislavski, who stated that tension usually has a focal point in the body, that it is different for each individual, and that it has the characteristic of "polluting" the entire body.

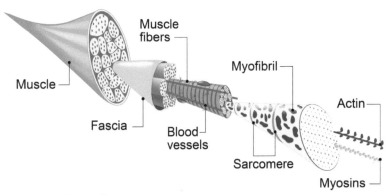

Constitution of muscle fibers

Muscle fibers
Myofibril
Actin
Muscle
Fascia
Blood vessels
Sarcomere
Myosins

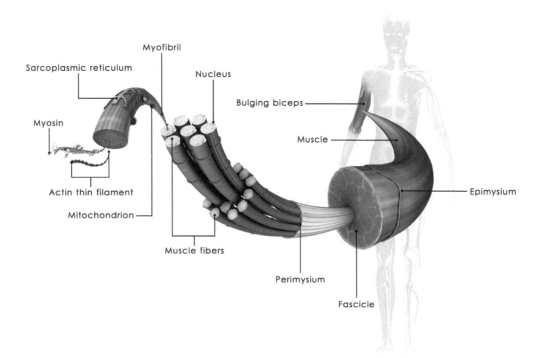

The German term *annspannung-abspannung* refers to the ebb and flow of muscular impulses and was used by Mary Wigman, pioneer of expressionist dance, as the foundation for dance theater principles in Europe. Wigman, a student of both Dalcroze and Laban, founded her own school in Dresden, Germany, around 1920. In Italy, where I was taught by Susanne Linke, a German choreographer and teacher, I learned a great deal about muscular control and awareness.

As noted in an article entitled "The Dynamo-Rhythm of Etienne Decroux and His Successors" that appeared in the August 2013 issue of *Mime Journal* (scholarship.claremont.edu/mimejournal; ISSN 2327–5650 online), the great mime Etienne Decroux took the particularly rich idea of comédie du muscle—muscular resistance—to locate the drama inside the muscle itself. Today we refer to mode tonique relâché, lâché, usuel, or détendu (tonic mode, relaxed, let go, usual gold, and relaxed gold). In mode tonique there was conflict, which of course projects a dramatic conflict, the actor's conflict, the actor's physiological conflict. It is the muscle structure that expresses the psychological conflict through the body. Decroux defined the theater as the place where drama is made, the place of conflict through opposing thoughts.

Here is the next key idea and set of questions we need to think about: How do we experience dance as audience members? How do we read "muscular drama"? How can we teach dance without knowing the process of metakinesis? What is kinesthesia?

The American dance critic John Martin wrote in his book *America Dancing*: "When we see a human body moving, we see movement which is potentially producible by a human body and therefore by our own; through kinesthetic sympathy we actually reproduce it vicariously in our present muscular experience and awaken such associational connotations as might have been ours if the original movement had been of our own making. The irreducible minimum of equipment demanded of a spectator, therefore, is a kinesthetic sense in working condition."

In her book *Choreographing Empathy*, Susan Lee Foster explains the relationship between the dance and the viewer:

> Now, at the beginning of the twenty-first century, neurophysiologists are claiming an intrinsic connectivity between dancer and viewer based on the discovery of the mirror neurons-synaptic connection in the cortex that fires both when one sees an action and when one does an action. ... To 'choreograph empathy' thus entails the construction and cultivation of a specific physicality whose kinesthetic experience guides our perception of and connection to what another is feeling. ... [The word] kinesthesia was coined in 1880, in response to a growing body of research establishing the existence of nerve sensors in the muscles and joints that provide awareness of the body's positions and movements. The meaning of the term has been expanded, abandoned, and revised several times over the course of the twentieth century."

In his book *Modern Dance Terminology*, Paul Love defines "metakinesis" as follows:

> The physical overtones accompanying movement; one of the four innovations of modern dance as listed by John Martin. Movement will without fail be colored by the personality of the person who produces it and will reflect his experience and temperament. Metakinesis is not different from but a part of the physical movement in the same sense that the body and the soul are two aspects of a single underlying reality. All movement is done with a purpose and is to some degree functional. It is the conscious recognition and use of this fact that distinguishes modern dance from other types.

In my search to better train and educate dancers and performers, I've always been eager to understand how other disciplines solve the same physical technical challenges. Throughout my career as a pedagogue, reading and researching anatomy, biomechanics, neuroscience, theater, mime, and choreography have opened my mind to different approaches and have provided me with different tools that I use to teach different kinds of performers and artists. I encourage all teachers to explore different disciplines that surround you and your context in order to make personal connections and build unique bridges of methodological approaches to educate and train yourself and/or your students.

The technical and consciousness training of performers consists of bridging two worlds: The inner and the outer, breath control and exploration (as modern dance pioneer Mary Wigman said, "breath connects the in- and outside worlds and environments), and muscular drama and kinesthetic empathy are the answers. How do performers or dancers see themselves from outside themselves? How do they want to be perceived? How do we bridge the gap between the emotion/feeling and the visual? We bridge it with years of meticulous training by mentors and other critical thinkers.

Dance as a Point of View

One article that I always give to my students is "Dance as a Point of View" by John Martin, who was lead dance critic at the *New York Times* for a long time and author of many books. In his article, he tries to define modern dance and how modern dance can be explained to an audience. He tries to define dance as a point of view on life. As Martin says, whatever you do, when you dance, teach dance, or choreograph, you are expressing a point of view about something. You are making and taking choices, and these choices inform your life philosophy, your unique point of view. Seeing someone's choreography or seeing a dancer's performance reveals a great deal about that person's personality, perhaps more so than

All Images: ALDD's Performance "Pachamama: Mother World" at Sheen Center, NYC, 2016

spoken language. Movement reveals who you are. When you see someone move—even just walking—you see what parts of the body they are comfortable with and which parts of the body they feel ashamed of. It seems to me that when you understand this notion of dance as a point of view on life, as a dancer, teacher, or choreographer, you start to understand the value of what you are doing.

A choreographer reveals their voice and point of view on life. Sometimes it is not conscious, and maybe it isn't until years later that you look at your own choreography and discover just how radical or superficial your point of view was. Consciously or not, you need to know that you are always expressing a point of view about something. This concept means that you are responsible for and consciousness of your artistic work.

I remember rehearsing my full-length piece *The Grass Is Always Greener*, which clearly expresses my point of view about immigration, particularly as it relates to the United States, but also in general. We were rehearsing to perform it outdoors. What was a five-woman show became a duet. At that time I was collaborating with the actor and theater director Daniel Pettrow, who came to rehearsal and coached me, saying, "Do not preach. Just communicate." That really struck me because in one way I was choreographing that show because I wanted to express my strong opinion. But Pettrow pointed out that if I started to preach, I would turn off the audience and the audience could easily leave the outdoor performance. He told me that if I were to focus on communicating my story, the point of view would be transmitted naturally. Sometimes a point of view is expressed not because you are screaming it but, rather, because you are whispering it.

But remember that your work is always a point of view.

The selection of material, the selection of movement, and the selection of props all express your point of view. Your artistic choices show what is important to you. In the process of creating *The Grass Is Always Greener*, I changed my approach and decided to ask the audience questions in the form of choreographic phrases about their own points of view on immigration in the past, present, and future.

"A bone to pick with you" performance at Crossroads Festival at Judson Church, NYC, 2021

When I see a choreographed work, it's hard for me to say "This is bad" or "This is good." I have come to understand that for me such statements refer to how well we define a point of view in our choreography. This understanding allows me to talk about the choreographic craft when I criticize it. For example, I might suggest that something needs more craft, that elements of time and space were underexplored, that the use of props or music was unattended to. This understanding allows me to give technical feedback about how a point of view is communicated rather than present a value judgment on the point of view itself. It annoys me when I see choreography whose choreographer is clearly unaware that they are expressing a point of view. I find this naïve. As artists, we are idealists, but we must not be naïve. We can be vulnerable but not dumb. A point of view comes across whether you want it to or not. To be unaware of this is naïve.

For me, choreography gives me agency.

Choreography is a capturing apparatus, a frame for my ideas and my lived existence as a mother, artist, and immigrant transplanted from South America to the United States.

Through choreography I try to capture the essence of my existence.

I became an American citizen in 2018. As the mother of a new generation of American citizens, my job is to nurture, protect, and guide. I offer and reinforce a critical thinking education through the arts and through dance.

As a citizen of the world, in my body the inside and outside worlds collide.

Both Images: "A bone to pick with you" performance at Crossroads Festival at Judson Church, NYC, 2021

Here is my Artist Statement:

Art is a political act.
Dance is discipline and revolt.
My body is my country.

I react to my environment and use the body as a receptacle for and messenger of the multiple realities that we are immersed in.

My work reflects my experience as a Latina artist living in New York and comes from a deep examination of my motivations as a woman, mother, and immigrant.

Performance is a conduit for examining cultural identity through form and content, as well as relationships between people and society.

Sharing my point of view of life with others is my duty and my pleasure.

I investigate the interior logic of performance and the role of the dancer in our culture today, redefining the parameters of dance and theater.

My works live inside and outside theatrical traditions and venues, as well as on the screen.

My art is about celebration and criticism of socio-political and cultural barriers. It is a ceremony of awareness.

I explore rituals to document intimacy, organize layers of character-driven drama, and break apart quotidian social gestures.

I am creating a living vocabulary of meaningful movement that springs directly from emotions with visceral strength.

By using movement, spoken word, sounds, music, photographs, video projections, film, masks, and props as tools, I create a dialogue to provoke a cathartic experience in the audience.

The principle that drives my work is that Motion Creates Emotion, and Emotion Creates Motion.

I love to work and collaborate in an atmosphere of creativity, respect, responsibility, honesty, independence, and freedom.

How to Communicate the Importance of Art, Performance, and Dance

As teachers, it's our responsibility to help our students and audiences understand how to talk about the importance of art, performance, and dance in our society and about the importance of the development of their careers in dance. Students need to know how to communicate about and advocate for the importance of art and dance in our society. Part of our mission is to introduce people to the arts and to establish and develop cultural, educational, and artistic exchanges between communities. Students need to understand that becoming arts advocates is part of their education.

Art, performance, and dance enrich people and communities,
transcending socio-political and cultural boundaries.

For 35 years, my mission has been to create an audacious and intimate choreographic language that opens a dialogue about creativity, memory, fantasy, reality, and social awareness within a global community.

A good example of this important skill comes from my own life. My parents always supported me in dance. They always said, "Whatever you want to do, you must do it one hundred percent." Growing up, I made my family part of my journey as a dancer and choreographer, sharing with them what I loved doing. I showed my parents videos of dance history, dance documentaries, and archival footage, and I asked them to watch me in classes and rehearsals (as well as my performances, of course). Happily, they came to understand what dance, performance, and choreography are and how much they mean to me. I felt it was my job to help them understand.

When I moved to the United States, my mom didn't want to talk to me for three months. She couldn't understand why I left, why I was leaving my family, my city, my country. She didn't understand why I left my dance company and the dance school I founded, which by then had 250 students. Why did I take the giant leap to remake myself and my life at 23 years old? It took years for them to start to understand my life choices.

From the intimacy of my family, my community, my hometown, my dance school, and my country, I expanded my sphere of interest and influence as it grew from a small circle to a large one. I believe it was part of my mission as an educator to advocate for the important role of the arts in society and the power of art to change lives for the better.

Artists and educators are agents of change.

Performance and dance are critical to the spread of empathy and acceptance of diversity. We must promote the flexibility of mind, body, and spirit.

"A bone to pick with you" performance at Crossroads Festival at Judson Church, NYC, 2021

PART II
LEARNING DANCE

"No More Beautiful Dances", Center for Performance Research, 2018

CHAPTER 8.
GUIDE TO THE BODY

In the following chapter, I provide a detailed review of certain fundamental physical principles that are especially important for us to be aware of as performers and dancers. I'll talk about anatomy, biomechanics, and energy, and about how they are related. Sometimes in teaching or learning dance, we fabricate relationships between different parts of the body that do not exist anatomically speaking. We connect parts of the body that aren't actually connected. As dancers we need to have knowledge of our anatomies as well as relevant imagery to understand how our bodies, our medium of expression, relates to life in performance.

Energy or Presence

Energy is how we make the invisible visible. Sometimes we forget that performance and dance are about communication. I am convinced that we have smaller and smaller audiences for the performing arts because choreographers, dancers, and performers are so removed from the principles of communicating.

By definition, we performers need an audience to make the invisible visible. The art, the magic, is made between performer and audience.

Energy is how we communicate. Energy is the bridge. As performers and dancers, we are the messengers, not the message.

In other cultures, this idea of energy in performance technique is called presence.

Examples include *kung-fu* in China; *prana* and *shakti* in India; *koshi*, *ki-hai*, and *yugen* in Japan; *chikara*, *taxu*, and *bayu* in Bali; and *animus* and *anima* in Roman times.

Two useful concepts, which we explore next, are identifying the center of energy and the projection of energy. We must define and master them to the best of our abilities and recognize how this energy is centered in our bodies while realizing energy's dependence on the performance mode, dance style, or technique used.

Let's define what energy is first!

In their *Dictionary of Theatre Anthropology: The Secret Art of the Performer*, Eugenio Barba and Nicola Savarese cite the *Penguin English Dictionary* published by Penguin Books in England in 1984: "Energy: power, force; capacity for doing work." Barba and Savarese go on to write that, "Performers' energy is a readily identifiable quality: It is the performer's nervous and muscular power. The mere fact that this power exists is not particularly interesting since it exists, by definition, in any living body. What is interesting is the way this power is molded in a very special context: the theater."

In *The Actor's Energy as Premise*, F. Taviani notes the following:

> The concept of energy … is a concept both obvious and difficult. We associate it with external impetus, with an excess of muscular and nervous activity. But it also refers to something intimate, something that pulses in immobility and silence, a retained power which flows in time without dispersing in space.

Energy is commonly reduced to imperious and violent behavior models, but it is actually a personal temperature-intensity which the performer can determine, awaken, mold and which above all needs to be explored.

The performer's extra-daily technique, their scenic presence, derives from an alteration of balance and basic posture, from the play of opposing tensions that dilate the body's dynamics.

The body is rebuilt for scenic fiction. This 'art body'—and therefore, 'unnatural body'—is neither male nor female. At the pre-expressive level, sex is of little import. Typical male energy and typical female energy do not exist.

There exists only an energy specific to a given individual.

The performer's task is to discover the individual propensities of his or her energy and to protect its potentialities, its uniqueness.

Center of Energy or of Movement

All techniques talk about the center of energy in the body, but too frequently we don't teach these principles to our students. This is problematic because if a dancer doesn't know where their center of energy is and where energy comes from, they will not know how to project it. This knowledge is essential for understanding how a performer communicates with the audience.

Different techniques place the center of energy in different parts of the body, depending on their philosophical and aesthetic point of view.

The first thing you need to identify and understand when you take or teach a dance technique class is where the center of energy is located.

The center of movement is the wellspring from which energy emerges in the body and spreads to all or some body parts.

In the past, different dance or performance techniques established different centers of movement, responding to specific philosophical and aesthetic points of view.

Tracing the evolution of dance and researching in dance history, we are aware of artists' deep investigation trying to decode why they move, how they move, and what makes them move.

In his book *Modern Dance Terminology*, Paul Love defines "center of movement" as "a central point within the body from which all movement is considered to spring. This central point is consciously felt by the dancer, whether outwardly expressed or not, and gives vitality to the movement."

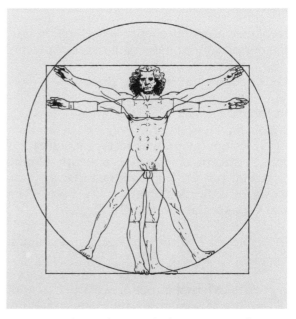

Vitruvian Man drawing by Leonardo da Vinci, c. 1490, illustrating the idea of kinesphere

76

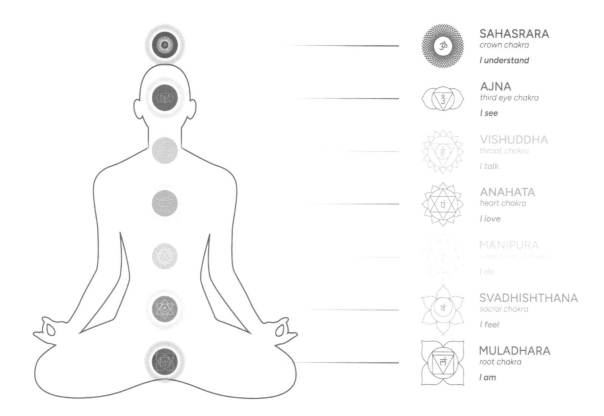

The seven Chakras

Paul Love writes:

Isadora Duncan has remarked that 'the ballet schools taught the pupils that this spring was found in the center of the back at the base of the spine.' From this axis, says the ballet master, arms, legs and trunk must move freely, giving the result of an articulated puppet. In academic ballet, the trunk was infrequently used. Because of the emphasis on leg movement, the lower center was most frequently used. It was Isadora Duncan who was to move this center to the upper body chest. 'For hours I would stand quite still,' she said, 'my two hands folded between my breasts, covering the solar plexus. I was seeking and finally discovered the central spring of all movements, the crater of motor power, the unity from which all diversities of movements are born.' This was one obvious disadvantage to the shift from the lower to an upper center, i.e., arms movement increased enormously while legs movement decreased.

The modern dance made the center somewhat more flexible. It may be shifted according to the type and quality of the movement desired, from the chest to the solar plexus, the pelvis, the base of the spine, etc. The center may also be arbitrarily chosen: that is, movements of the arm, when the figure is in a crouched sitting position, may be made to appear in their action to be expelled from the pelvis as center. The use of any desired portion of the trunk as center allows both arms and legs to be used equally.

Other examples of where the spine is the center of movement are classical ballet, Merce Cunningham, and the Lester Horton technique.

In West African dances and Humphrey-Limón techniques, there are two centers of movement: the heart chakra and what is called "the diamond," which is located between the navel and the pubic bone.

In contemporary dance or hip hop, there are eclectic systems in which the center of movement moves freely to different body parts according to the movements. That is why these types of dancers can create isolated or dislocated movements. They are transferring the center of energy or movement to different body parts as they dance.

Because of my own training, I tend to use three different centers of energy, depending on what kind of choreographic investigation I'm working with. One center of energy is the spine, which I imagine to be like a fluorescent light through which energy passes, moving up through the atlas vertebra at the top of the head (what I call "la fontanella" or fountain, like a whale's spout) and down through the tailbone. The spine is an *axis mundi*, connecting paradise above to hell below. Another image that I use is that of a drinking straw, where energy travels up and down like a liquid.

In history and art, vivid images of the axis of the universe vary widely, since they depend on the culture's particular worldview. None of these images has a static function. They are all places of active passage and transition. As places of dynamic union where beings of quite different natures come together or pass into one another, the images of *axis mundi* may be associated with the coincidence of opposites. An example that I like to use in my classes is a cosmic tree, at whose top abides the celestial divinity. It is another frequent image standing for the axis of the world. The roots of the cosmic tree may sink into the underworld while its branches traverse the multiple world planes.

What are chakras in yoga? There are seven wheels of energy in the body that start at the crown of your head and travel down the body to the base of your spine. When spinning properly, each chakra allows Qi energy to flow through the body.

The second center of energy, the heart chakra, is located on the sternum, the same position as in yoga (see Chakra image on page 77).

The heart chakra serves as our center of love for oneself and others, compassion, empathy, and forgiveness. This chakra is associated with unconditional love and joy. It is the source of deep and profound truths that cannot be expressed in words.

The heart chakra is used as a center of movement in Humphrey-Limón and François Delsarte techniques in different ways. In addition to the physical, this center of energy also strongly reflects the emotional sphere. Because my dance practices explore the principle "Motion creates emotion, and emotion creates motion," the heart chakra is very active in my dance.

This principle goes hand in hand with Delsarte's concept "Every gesture is expressive of something. … It is preceded by and given birth by a thought, a feeling, an emotion, a purpose, a design or a motive."

The third center of energy I like to think of as "the diamond," which is located between the navel and the pubic bone, where the sexual organs exist. It's not just the uterus. It's all of the sexual energy embodied in that space and is also sometimes called "the creativity center." In yoga it is called "the sacral chakra" and represents creativity, sensuality, fertility of ideas, and sexual flow. This center holds the microbiome, the gut.

Where the center of energy is affects how one moves and projects energy into space.

In my barre à terre or ballet classes, I explain that the spine is the center of movement. It is where light emerges and spreads energy to the arms, head, and legs. The arms are anatomically connected to the fourth dorsal vertebra (T4), through which passes the spinal cord, the center of the nervous system. If you injure your T4, you will feel a tickling in the arms and will be unable to lift them. The T4 is exactly where energy in the spine connects with the arms and extends to the middle fingers, projecting energy into space.

The third lumbar vertebra (L3) is where nerves in the spine connect to the legs. If you experience any injury to the L3 vertebra—whether it's sciatica, a pinched vertebra, or something else—you will be unable to lift your leg.

If we overlay the maps of how energy moves through the spine that are commonly seen in Asian (meridian lines) and Western medicine traditions, we see that both point to approximately the same vertebrae as centers of movement or energy. The L3 vertebra carries energy, an imaginary light, from your spine to your legs, particularly to the posterior fascia and heels. Similarly, energy passes from the spine through the top of the head from the first cervical vertebra, or the atlas.

So, the first thing we need to do for ourselves when we enter a dance technique class is to understand where the center of movement is for that particular technique. This knowledge is as fundamental as knowing your roots and origins, which country and city you're from, and your family members' names. Without understanding the center of movement, you are unable to fully embody movement. You will be able only to repeat phrases of choreography like a parrot. Many times, unfortunately, dance teachers themselves aren't aware of where the center of movement is in the technique they teach.

Investigating this body/energy relationship for the past 35 years as I strove to improve my practice and my teaching, I encountered an article entitled "Reading the Body in Dance" by Hubert Godard, a Rolf Movement Practitioner and certified Rolfer since 1986. He is a member of the Rolf Institute and has taught Rolfing for over 20 years. Since 1988, Godard has been a researcher for the National Institute for Cancer Research in Milan, Italy. In 1990, he was appointed Director for the Dance and Movement Analysis Department of the University of Paris, where he still teaches movement analysis.

I find Godard's insights put forth at a symposium at the University of Paris in 1987 meaningful:

> We will take the spine as the starting point, but 'spine' in the largest sense, as an image that includes mechanics, relationship and symbolism. The function of the spine will be understood as the capacity to perceive and respond to two fields, two polarities – in a way, the spine will be understood as a movement.
>
> First gravity, the perception of weight: Do we feel the weight of our body from the top down? This will allow us to be gravid, to 'give birth' to a second, opposing direction, called anti-gravitational or lengthening or syntropic (as opposed to entropic): a kind of life force. This second, upward movement will always keep the memory of the one who gave it birth, just as the way we hold ourselves echoes the way that we have been held. This is the image of the Tao: human being suspended between earth and sky, in perpetual relation with one and the other.
>
> The quality of perception and relationship with these two fields is our foundation; it creates our autonomy. In a close analogy, breathing plays between these two fields, inspiration and upward movement, expiration and movement down.

Projection of Energy

Once we understand the concept of center of energy/movement, we can begin to think about how we project energy into the kinesphere and into physical space.

Dance technique was born to prepare the body to be on stage, often in huge opera houses around the world, not just small dance studios like we have in New York City. Knowing this, we need to train our energy like an actor or an opera singer trains their voice to project into space so we can reach out to, communicate with, and emote to the audience.

From the center of movement, energy travels to the different body parts. Then, through our movement, this energy goes out into physical space. By amplifying sound, the audience is able to hear better. Similarly, the idea is that by projecting energy, you amplify your internal character into space.

It sometimes seems to me that young dancers tend to be self-indulgent in their performance choices. They dance because it feels good and their goal seems to be self-satisfaction. Of course, it is true that dancing feels fantastic, but to become a professional this is not enough. Most dancers probably don't want to dance for themselves in their living rooms their whole lives! I presume they want to dance and perform because dance is, after all, a form of art and communication. An artist gives generously and thus moves beyond self-indulgent performance.

Energy projection depends in part on muscular tension, the use of "muscular drama," which I discussed earlier. There is often confusion about the distinction between energy and muscular tension. Tension is the accumulation of energy within the body, which must be conscious. Too often it is not conscious, which does not serve our purposes as dancers. For example, if you need to develop a character who is frantic or explosive, you work on accumulating energy in your spine and directing it inward, building tension.

We need to understand that it can be good to have tension in your body, but you also need to know how to release energy accumulated in tension. Both shape your stage presence differently.

One exercise I use to practice this awareness of tension is to ask students to imagine that they are balloons full of air and then that someone is poking holes in different parts of the balloon, releasing air. The air escaping the balloon is tension releasing. This exercise helps to make the invisible idea of tension visible.

The projection of energy goes hand in hand with breath as well. Breath helps us regulate the degree of freedom with which energy flows. What you want to do will determine how you use your breath and thus how your energy flows into space.

In my teaching, I prefer to always integrate elements of performance technique into physical technique classes, even for amateurs. My philosophy is that we never know what the student will end up doing, so I'd rather prepare them to be a professional dancer so they know how to move their body and project energy. Whether the student ends up using that tool or not, at least they have access to it.

All Images: "Listen to Your Mother" performance at Movement Research at Judson Church, NYC, 2023

The Three Circles of Energy Method

I like to use a specific exercise in my classes to address the idea of performance and projection of energy in conjunction with physical technique. The book *The Second Circle: How to Use Positive Energy for Success in Every Situation* by Patsy Rodenburg inspired my teaching and artistic practices.

Patsy Rodenburg began to recognize the different types of energy that a human being can learn to harness: energy of the body, the breath, the voice, the mind, the heart, and the spirit. We all give out energy, and by listening we all receive energy. Rodenburg identifies three basic movements of energy (which I discuss in greater detail below):

The **first circle** is inward-moving, drawing energy toward the self. At the opposite extreme is the **third circle**, in which energy is forced outward toward the world at large. In the **second circle**, energy is focused on a specific object or person and moves in both directions: taking in and giving out. The second circle is intimate and might make you think of the saying "the eyes are the windows of the soul."

According to Rodenburg, "Presence is the energy that comes from you and connects you to the outside world. It is essential to your survival when you are threatened. It is the heart intimacy between people, and although you can live in your inner world without presence in yourself, the outer world we live in will appear dull, stale, and flat. It is when you are fully present that you do your best work and make your deepest impression."

I compare the circles of energy to a camera lens that zooms in and out. I explain it to my students this way: Imagine a wide angle picture in which you see a couple in the distance kissing at sundown in a beautiful landscape, their silhouettes against the horizon. Now imagine zooming in, so you can see the bodies of the couple and can recognize their faces, clothes, etc. Zoom in even closer to see just their faces, their lips, hands running through their hair. The circles of energy are like zooming in and out, where each circle reveals and provides different opportunities to the audience. It's a continuum where the performer chooses to show intimate details or exposes the audience to a wider view of the overall performance.

If you've ever driven a manual car, you know that you have to shift the gears up and down to get where you're going. With this idea in mind, you can see there are different ways to perform a phrase of movement. One can perform a physical movement in different ways by manipulating the projection of energy and using the three circles of energy. We can project energy in different ways to communicate different ideas with the same movements.

The success of a performance depends on the awareness of how we project energy. If an actor performs a monologue with introspective energy (first circle) for an hour, the audience will probably quickly become bored. A good actor might mumble to himself as a tool for a minute, but would later change the way he projects his energy to continue communicating with his audience and to make the material interesting to watch.

The Three Circles of Energy method helps us cultivate awareness of these different degrees of energy projection.

First Circle – The first circle of energy represents self-knowledge and introspection. Projection of energy into the first circle will communicate personal, self-reflective ideas to the spectator. In essence, you feel your body moving but do not care who is watching you. The energy is directed inward, just you with yourself. This is an important circle to be aware of as it can be useful, but some types of dancers often tend to live entirely in this first circle, which limits what they can communicate. Ask yourself to develop a consciousness of what it feels and looks like to perform movements with this type of first circle introspective energy.

Second Circle – This circle of energy represents the exchange of energy with another performer, audience, music, prop, etc. The exchange is evident. The audience witnesses this exchange unless the second circle of energy is between the performer and the audience. It is the energy and awareness of a pas de deux, a duet. Your intention is reactive to the different environments that you are immersed in. The second circle of energy is being aware and open to give and receive. The joy of life and performance happens in this circle.

Third Circle – The third circle of energy helps you to project energy indiscriminately outward. Politicians and religious leaders often use this third circle of energy to make their presence bigger, limitless, and constant. It is the energy that you project when you are dancing a solo on the biggest stage imaginable and everyone, even people sitting in the very last row of the balcony must be able to see what you are doing. In classical ballet, the third circle is used most of the time. Practice projecting this energy in various scenarios, with various audience sizes and different size spaces. This circle of projection is not directed to a single object or person. It is to the masses, as if you are speaking or performing for 10,000 people. The intention is to be heard, and you do not focus on a specific individual in the audience. When you project an intense energy outward in this way, the other thing that happens is that you simultaneously create protection around yourself, like a forcefield or shield against external forces.

I apply this methodology in all my ballet, modern dance, and dance theater classes to teach students how to understand their presence and how the audience perceives them. Of course, it goes beyond teaching and is an essential creative tool I use in all my rehearsals and choreographic productions.

Performance for me is like kissing a new boyfriend or girlfriend while your old boyfriend or girlfriend is watching you! You are aware that your old partner is watching you, and you are provoking them in a sly, coquettish way. Sometimes your attention goes to the lips and tongue of the new partner, and sometimes you become lost in the moment, feeling your own lips and tongue. And sometimes your attention goes to showing all of this to the old boyfriend or girlfriend. Performance involves changing circles, changing perception, changing awareness of presence so that it's fun to experience for both the performer and the audience!

Gravity and Balance

Once we understand the concept of center of energy, we can then differentiate between center of movement and center of gravity. The center of gravity (COG) refers to how the body's weight interacts with the force of gravity. The COG does not change across techniques, whereas the center of energy might. The COG is located between the belly button and the sacrum—right in the middle of your body—but take note: It is not a fixed point!

The COG of the human body is a hypothetical point around which the force of gravity appears to act. It is a point at which the combined mass of the body appears to be concentrated. It is the place through which you most feel the effects of gravity, the downward pull or force that the earth exerts on your body, thereby giving you weight. COG is the point around which a body's weight is equally balanced in all directions.

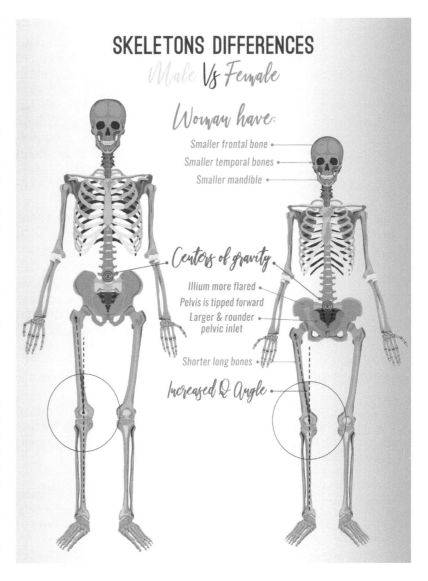

Skeletons Differences, Male Vs. Female

When we define the COG, we do so from the reference of a static, standing position. However, the body is almost continuously in motion, which means it often changes position. With each new position comes a new location for the COG. Remember, the center of gravity is the point around which all the parts balance. Regardless of which dance technique or style we practice, the concept of gravity must be comprehended and analyzed for us to master body control.

Modern dance pioneer Doris Humphrey investigated the concept of what she termed "fall and recovery" and how gravity is a philosophical synonymous or adverse force. Humphrey was interested in the fundamental importance of tension and relaxation in the body, and she used it as the foundation for her own system of movement principles. The breath cycle was a system of "fall and recovery," for example, and her vocabulary was based on the notion that all movement patterns followed suit, including opposition, succession, and unison. She codified this system, and her assistant, Ernestine Stodelle, wrote a book entitled *The*

Dance Technique of Doris Humphrey and Its Creative Potential (1978), expanding on these ideas. I trained and studied at Limón Institute in New York City with many master teachers of the Humphrey-Limón technique for many years. I highly recommend that dancers, no matter what discipline they follow, spend time training in this technique to master gravity and rhythm of breath.

The American choreographer Elizabeth Streb also investigates how "invisible forces," such as gravity, centrifugal force, inertia, etc., affect the human's body movements. Gravity is something that we have to fight with. In her book entitled *How to Become an Extreme Action Hero* (2010), Streb crystallizes her investigations in this field. Streb has been pushing the limits of the human body with the development of her movement technique, PopAction, for decades. In 2003 she established S.L.A.M. (STREB Lab for Action Mechanics), a factory space in Williamsburg, Brooklyn, which produces extreme action performances and offers training classes for adults and kids.

Streb wrote the following in her book:

> Meet the monster, the ugly part of our world—gravity—and all its other force-field friends: inertia, rebound, impact, adhesion, centripetal force, momentum, velocity, acceleration, and dead stops.

> This thing called gravity is what all motion genres avoid even acknowledging; certainly dance, ballet, and the circus spend a lot of time camouflaging its effect. Only football, rodeo, boxing, and World Wrestling Entertainment are un-afraid of this force, the weakest one we have on earth.

> …[E]xercises serve a purpose: they increase the range, speed, and accuracy of the body that chooses to move. You have to get the muscles onto the correct spot on your skeleton so there is no motion impeded by a muscle mass. Your joints become fully free.

Doris Humphrey's technique defines "fall and recovery" as metaphors for life and death. Dance (movement) is the arc between these two extremes. Gravity is a symbol for all problems in society, so in order for the human to survive, it must arise from gravity.

As Isadora Duncan said, "All movement on earth is governed by the law of gravitation, by attraction and repulsion, resistance and yielding; it is that which makes up the rhythm of the dance."

For me, simply being vertical is a statement in itself. When you stand up vertically in performance, you make a statement in your act against gravity. Anytime we move, our mind, body, and spirit make choices about how we relate to gravity. The presence of gravity affects how much tension or relaxation our muscles experience and how much energy we do or don't use. These physical concepts relate to larger spiritual questions about how we relate to gravity and how gravity informs our point of view in life. Different techniques and art practices take different approaches to gravity.

Sometimes, even gravity informs us about our emotional experiences. Resistance comes into play here. We all experience feelings of needing to resist something. Isn't this the nature of political art? Isn't art sometimes a rebellion against the system that oppresses and holds you down?

When I train and perform, I am always aware of this polarity, this connection with the earth, and the fact that I am between the sky and the earth is what dance is about.

As I mentioned before, for me the spine is the *axis mundi* that connects them both.

Whether you are studying dance, performing, or teaching, I implore you to take time to think about all the different techniques and styles of dance, different modes of performance, and how they address gravity and verticality. In your mind's eye, scan the body like an X-ray to understand the techniques' points of view on life.

Left and Right Page: Fiamma Lenzu-Carroll performing "Once upon a Dance," New York Live Arts, NYC, 2023

When we are vertical, we are simultaneously between two worlds, in a muscular dramatic state.

Growing up as an Argentinian-Italian Catholic and surrounded by images that depict heaven and earth, I always imagined that above us is paradise and below us is hell. We are in purgatory, between paradise and hell. I cannot deny the influence of Dante's *Divine Comedy*!

Dance is a state of being in an "in-between place." The dancer is in motion, in fluctuation between up and down, always dealing with gravity. That is why I say that movement defies gravity. Movement defines the most profound problem of society that each person embodies, the conflict between life and death, as Doris Humphrey says.

I was about 23 years old when I discovered the Humphrey-Limón technique. Ideas of fall and recovery, falling in a spiral, and falling backward all just clicked for me. I immediately understood that my choices in opposition to verticality—the *axis mundi*—determined how I would move. We are always moving in and out of balance. Even walking is a fall and recovery action against gravity. It is the dance of balance/imbalance.

The Humphrey-Limón technique creates these muscular tensions or "muscular dramas," moving between being off-balance and in balance. It's actually pretty boring when a trained dancer stays in perfect balance. It is the vulnerability of the dancer moving between being in balance and off-balance that is interesting. It is the vulnerability of the dancer choosing to give up certain things or not. This game embodies and captures the essence of life. Living the present in each choice.

The relationship to gravity is also a psychological experience. Psychologically, in our act of resisting gravity as dancers, we are literally opposing a system. We are resisting and asking questions about the way things are. As dancers we train and fortify our ability to resist gravity. That is what we do. When you begin training, the most difficult thing to accomplish is moving from standing, down to the floor, and back up again. How we do it depends on choreography, of course. The hardest dance movement isn't actually jumping. Of course, jumping is difficult, especially the big leaps, but moving to the floor and then back to standing is even more so. Again, it's all about this game of being in balance and being off balance. When you are off balance you are searching for balance. You are asking questions. That is life. If we think that we are always on balance, where is the fun in that? The search for physical, emotional, spiritual, social, and economic balance is the challenge for any artist, especially the performers!

Why Must You Study Barre à Terre?

Technique equals control. In the academic ballet technique, $2 + 2 = 4$. You must resist gravity, project energy into space, use rotation and opposition. By working with an economy of energy and movement you discover how to work using your muscle tone. I want people to work with joy, to explore and learn how to use their bodies and energies efficiently and healthily as instruments of expression. In my class, dancers increase their flexibility and strength, and they acquire the muscular awareness to prevent injuries and overcome physical difficulties, incorrect posture, or alignment.

My greatest satisfaction comes from seeing dancers discover their own potential. For me, teaching is showing myself just as I am. I practically grew up teaching dance, so it feels natural for me. I teach dance to professionals and amateurs the same. I embrace and encourage them equally. Everyone receives the same information, passion, love, and respect. **Dance is a means, not an end.**

In 2006, I began to systematically teach what I call Structural Barre à Terre. Thinking about what kind of complementary training dancers needed for strengthening, increasing flexibility and sensitivity, and educating their bodies, no matter their technique, I considered new tools I might provide and new approaches in my teaching.

My classes are for people who wish to explore and learn about the fundamentals of their bodies' functionality, bring awareness to their movement and their dancing, learn to use their bodies in service of movement, and become receptive to changes.

On the floor, under the effect of gravity, you become aware of the conscious and unconscious uses of energy and musculature: You can isolate and explore the functions of different parts of the body and their proper use. It takes patience and consistency to achieve an honest and available body. As Doris Humphrey said, "You have to learn to make your body transparent and translucent, so that emotions and ideas can pass freely and naturally."

Top and Middle: Anabella teaching at Peridance Center, NYC, 2018

Bottom: Anabella teaching at Peridance Center, NYC, 2019

Make the body available. The body is the means, not the end!

It is difficult to leave ego and resistance aside, but open-mindedness is crucial. Every technique requires this, but with barre à terre, I offer an appropriate time and space in which to achieve it. No stress, no limits, no self-judgment.

Movement springs from the inside and manifests itself externally. Actors, dancers, singers, musicians, painters. Anybody can take my class. Although their reasons for taking my class may differ, they all have one reason in common: self-discovery.

Alignment, Neutral Spine, Bones, Energy, and Fascia

What is alignment? Why do we need alignment in order to move and perform?

Alignment is the organization of energy in the body, as well as the bones and muscles. For energy to pass freely through the body, your bones, muscles, tendons, ligaments, and fascia must be aligned in such a way that allows this to happen. We work on physical alignment so that the path of energy can move freely like a river. Sometimes a choreographer will ask you to block energy in some part of your body, or a theater director may ask you to create a particular character who experiences certain types of energy blockage, in which case you will move out of alignment to achieve this goal.

If you organize your entire body energetically, your muscles will work properly and without extra effort or excess, and your joints will move freely.

Have you ever seen a film of a cheetah running at full speed? Why is it the fastest animal on earth? These films often show the cheetah running in slow motion, and you can observe how relaxed the muscles look and their nearly perfect body mechanics. For energy to pass freely, joints need to move freely.

When we use the right amount of energy, movement happens effortlessly. Imagine that you are wearing soaking wet clothes, a heavy cotton sweater and pants. You will feel the weight of the wet fabric hanging off you. In a completely relaxed and passive state, your muscles hang from the structure of your bones if there is no accumulation of tension (extra energy). Keep in mind, however, that your bones float inside your muscles (this is an anatomical fact!). Movement happens when you move bone articulations, letting energy pass.

How I teach alignment to my students depends completely on their backgrounds, physical training, and experience. The way I explain alignment to a dancer differs from the way I explain it to a musician, an actor, or an opera singer.

There are many ways to approach the topic: For example, to a child or young adult I will talk about the spine and the bones, constitution, and alignment. The whole conversation begins with anatomy, bone structure, and facts about bones, instead of going directly to the imagination, as many dance teachers do. Why? Because I want young people to understand the beautiful and perfect machine that is the human body. In this way they become conscientious of their instrument of expression, as a violinist is aware of the musical instrument.

With students who are mature and intellectually curious, I start talking about energy and projection of energy in the kinesphere and physical space.

Another approach is to delve deeper into the facts about bones, such as:

- You have 206 bones in your body.
- Your bones are the levers of your muscles.
- Some bones protect internal organs like the brain, lungs, heart, and sexual organs.
- Your bones store and release minerals like calcium and fat.
- Some bones produce red blood cells.
- Your muscles are attached to your bones by tendons.
- Ligaments connect bone to bone.
- Specific movement depends on the type of joint, such as the ball-and-socket joints in your shoulders and hips.
- There are 26 bones in the human foot.
- The periosteum is the sheath outside your bones that supplies them with blood, nerves, and the cells that help them grow and heal.
- **Bone Remodeling:** The body's skeleton forms and grows to its adult size in a process called modeling. The skeleton then completely regenerates—or remodels—itself roughly every 10 years. Remodeling removes old pieces of bone and replaces them with new, fresh bone tissue. This process keeps the bone and its cells healthy and strong, and it allows the bones to supply calcium to the body.
- Bone mass in the skeleton makes up about 14% of the total body weight (about 10–11 kg for an average person). Your muscles weigh approximately 50% of your total body weight. This means that bones are lighter than muscles.
- Bone is not uniformly solid but consists of a flexible matrix (about 30%) and bound minerals (about 70%), which are intricately woven and continuously remodeled by a group of specialized bone cells. Their unique composition and design allow bones to be relatively hard and strong while remaining lightweight.

Concept of Neutral Spine

Your spine is capable of flexion, extension, side-bending, rotation, and variations of all these combined. Your intervertebral discs cushion your vertebrae with curves. You have four curves in your spine acting like springs on a mattress: two are concave (cervical and lumbar) and two are convex (thoracic and sacral curves). See Spine illustration page 96.

In the standing position, a neutral spine is the alignment of the hip points (anterior superior iliac spine) and the pubis in the same vertical plane with the head stacked on the spine.

A fundamental component of maintaining a neutral spine is having a strong set of core muscles. Strong core muscles can help keep your spine naturally aligned and protected from impact.

To achieve a neutral spine, lie down on the floor with your back against the floor. Keep your head balanced and relax the muscles on the front and back of your neck. Make sure the back of your lungs and ribs touch the floor without downward pressure on the lumbar curve of the spine. In this position, it's important to respect the natural curve of the lumbar vertebrae. Your sacrum, like a rice bowl, is balancing and touching the floor. Don't tuck or tilt your hip!

Practicing your posture with a neutral spine, you will understand how muscles work without overworking them, liberating your joints and protecting the spine from risky movement or strong impact.

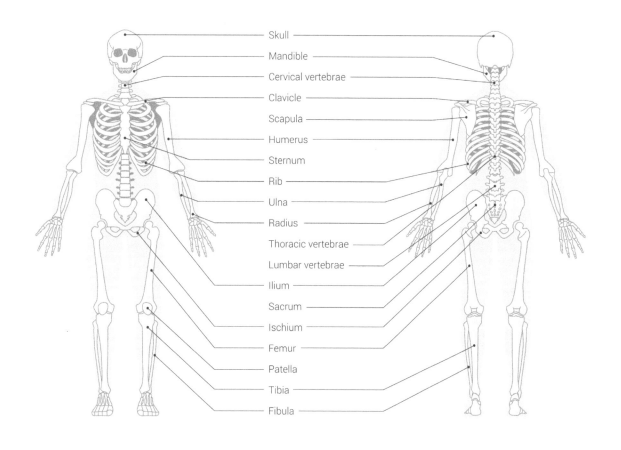

Skull

Mandible

Cervical vertebrae

Clavicle

Scapula

Humerus

Sternum

Rib

Ulna

Radius

Thoracic vertebrae

Lumbar vertebrae

Ilium

Sacrum

Ischium

Femur

Patella

Tibia

Fibula

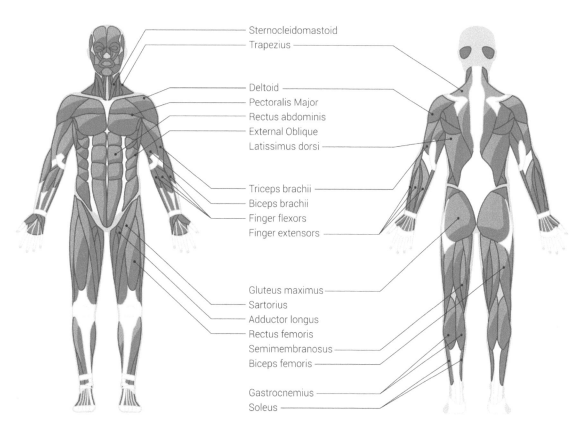

Sternocleidomastoid

Trapezius

Deltoid

Pectoralis Major

Rectus abdominis

External Oblique

Latissimus dorsi

Triceps brachii

Biceps brachii

Finger flexors

Finger extensors

Gluteus maximus

Sartorius

Adductor longus

Rectus femoris

Semimembranosus

Biceps femoris

Gastrocnemius

Soleus

The directional pull of gravity on your body can be represented by an imaginary vertical line, called the line of gravity or plumb line. For ideal alignment, your bones, not your muscles, should carry most of your body weight. Each body part should be properly balanced over the part below it.

Depending on the student, I teach neutral spine awareness by having them lie down on the floor, stand against the wall, or just stand up in the center of the room.

You must apply a neutral spine in almost all dance techniques used for the stage!

When I teach pre-professionals, I address awareness about muscular use, energy, and the connection of fascia so they understand alignment. I want these students to give deep care and attention to their instrument of expression. I want them to understand how to improve, maintain, train, and preserve the body so they can be healthy and keep dancing for a long time into the future!

What Is Fascia?

Fascia is a thin casing of connective tissue that surrounds and holds every organ, blood vessel, bone, nerve fiber, and muscle in place. The tissue does more than provide internal structure: Fascia has nerves that make it almost as sensitive as skin. When stressed, it tightens up.

In his book *Anatomy Trains*, Tom Myers writes this about the fascia:

> These sheets and lines follow the warp and weft of the body's connective tissue fabric, forming traceable 'meridians' of myo-fascia. Stability, along with strain, tension, fixation, resilience, and – most pertinent to this text – postural compensation, are all distributed be derived via these lines.

> … In order to progress, contemporary therapists need to think 'outside the box' of this isolated muscle concept. Research supporting this kind of systemic thinking will be cited along the way as we work our way through the implications of moving beyond the 'isolated muscle' to see systemic effects. This book is an attempt to move ahead – not to negate, but to complement the standard view– by assembling linked myofascial structures in this image of the 'myo-fascial meridians.'

> The word 'meridian' is usually used in the context of the energetic lines of transmission in the domain of acupuncture. Let there be no confusion: the myofascial meridian lines are not acupuncture meridians, but lines of pull, based on standard Western anatomy, lines which transmit strain and movement through the body's myo-fascia around the skeleton.

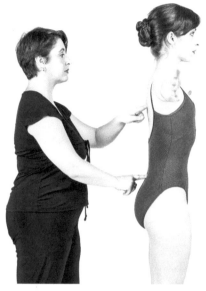

Left: Anabella explains the neutral spine. Lauren Ohmer, dancer, 2015
Right: Anabella teaching at Peridance Center, NYC, 2019

TYPES OF STANDING POSTURE

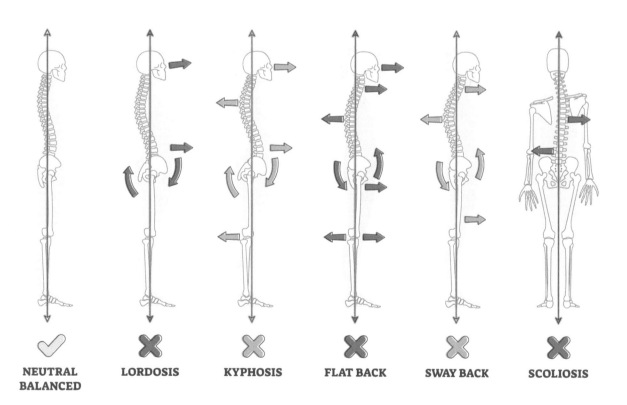

NEUTRAL BALANCED   LORDOSIS   KYPHOSIS   FLAT BACK   SWAY BACK   SCOLIOSIS

First Alignment, Then Movement

When we first learn to move, we usually start by copying movements from outside, by copying shapes. When you learn the alphabet as a child, you learn by copying the patterns and shapes of the letters. The same thing happens with dancing, especially if you start when you're little. For the very young, it's hard to understand anatomy and body structure. However, young students must learn about anatomical principles, energy, center of energy, gravity, balance, tension, and muscular drama. It is not something a student should discover for the first time in adolescence. These concepts must be introduced as early as possible, keeping in mind the methodology and didactic application to the specific age, body experience, and training.

In my years of teaching pre-professional and intermediate-level dancers, I have consistently found that these concepts are rarely talked about in dance class. Too often, student training is simple repetition of the teacher's steps, like a parrot repeating nonsense words. It's no wonder dance instruction is confusing and frustrating for students in this situation. The teacher provides imagery that is difficult to absorb without related background information and without anatomical knowledge. During an ideal training process, on the other hand, the dancer envisions his or her entire body and the relationships between different body parts—head, torso, spine, arms, legs, hips, etc.

When I'm teaching and I see a dancer with a lot of tension in the jaw, cheeks, or forehead, I read these signs like a thermometer for the entire body. If the body is tense, you'll see it in the face, the lips, the cheeks, and the eyes. You'll see a locked expression. When we block the passage of energy through the spine, the entire body tenses.

When I help a student get into alignment to allow energy to pass freely, I ask them to start by feeling their line of gravity or plumb line. (See drawings on page 93.) Like a bricklayer building a perpendicular wall, the "weight" tool is like the plumb line for a dancer or performer.

Straight lines are easier to understand physically than curves, especially in kids. You need to start with straight lines, progress to curves, then move to combining them. It is much easier to organize the body into a straight line and in symmetry, even though we know that we don't have perfectly symmetrical faces, and the right and left sides of our bodies are not perfectly symmetrical. One important goal of performance training is to strive for equal development of both sides, muscularly and energetically. This is extremely important to help prevent injuries!

I started my ballet training at six years old. What I loved first about ballet were simply the beautiful lines of the bodies and the movement that dancers traced in space. Ballet works expressly with symmetry, balance, and equilibrium, following the Greek idea of connecting the concepts of Apollo (order) and Dionysus (chaos). To create art, we need both order and chaos, light and dark, straight lines and curved lines, alignment and disorder.

The first step toward embodying all of these dichotomies is understanding how energy can flow as freely as possible in straight lines through the body, how to organize the body to allow that passage of energy, and how to break apart this organization.

Dance and performance master order and chaos, fluctuating from alignment to disorder. We need both, but we will never master our movements without being aware of alignment. First alignment, then movement.

Anatomical Knowledge

In this section, I begin to dive into the specifics of how we achieve physical and energy alignment to make our bodies available for self expression.

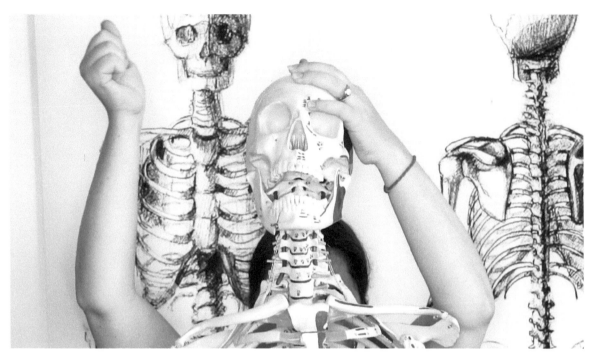

Screenshot from dance film "Close to the Bone," Brooklyn, 2022

Spine, Head, and Coccyx

Your Spine

The spine, as we've briefly discussed in earlier sections, is the center of energy and movement accessed most commonly through different techniques.

The spine is composed of 33 vertebrae that connect the skull, shoulders, ribs, hips, and legs. The vertebrae protect and surround the spinal cord. The spinal cord is a long, tube-like band of tissue. It connects your brain to your lower back. Your spinal cord carries nerve signals from your brain to your body and vice versa. These nerve signals help you feel sensations and move your body.

We have four curves in the spine: the cervical, the thoracic or dorsal, the lumbar, and the sacral curve. The curves, along with intervertebral disks, work to absorb and distribute stresses that occur when we perform everyday activities.

When you lie down on the ground, a common misconception is that your spine should lie flat on the ground, removing any curves of the spine. This is almost never true. Some individuals' body structures may have less lumbar and cervical curve in their spines so they can lie on the floor with nearly flat backs. Others, especially those with lordosis, will experience more accentuated curves in the spine when lying on the floor. But rarely if ever

Spine

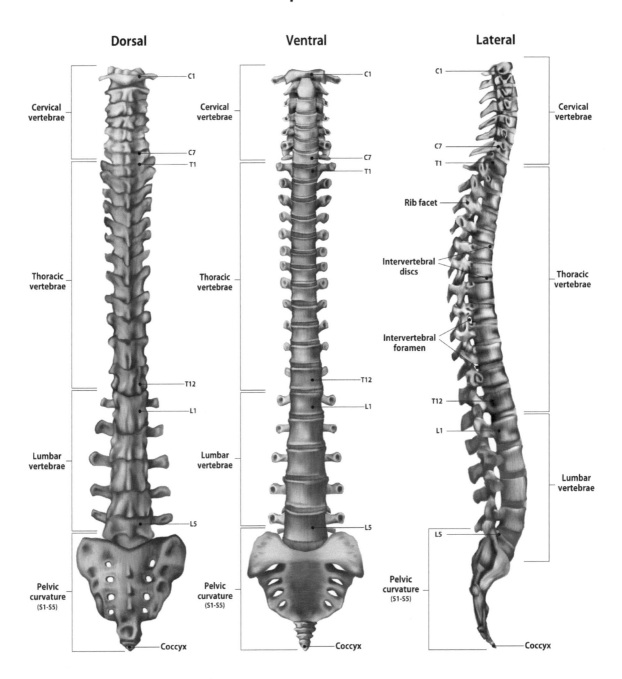

does anyone's spine naturally flatten on the ground. If you try to press your lumbar vertebrae on the ground to flatten the lumbar curve, you're actually moving the pelvis forward or tucking the pelvis inward so the pubic bone is pointing toward the ceiling. We do not want that! As we discussed in the previous chapter on Alignment (pages 93-94), to achieve proper alignment we have to work on our neutral spine.

I typically explain to my students that we want to imagine that the whole spine is like a necklace made of pearls on an elastic band. When you pull the elastic, the pearls (or vertebrae) separate to allow mobility between the vertebrae. We know that the entire flexibility and expressiveness of the body depends on the flexibility of our spine. So, if some areas of the spine are blocked or have little mobility, the energy cannot pass freely from the body to your kinesphere or the physical space you're dancing in. Just as we don't want to over-flatten the spinal curves, we also don't want to over-accentuate them. We must make the body available, as Doris Humphrey said, and put our bodies in a transparent, available state where ideas, thoughts, and emotion can flow freely!

It is important to imagine a lengthening of the spine to soften these spinal curves, rather than pinching the vertebrae together. Our aim is to relax the superficial muscles and create a loose separation of the vertebrae from one another. At all costs, we must not pinch the vertebrae together in an exaggerated fashion for the misleading notion of "economy of energy"—that is, to use the least amount of energy possible to execute a movement. You want to use your muscles with the least stress and effort possible to avoid overworking the joints. The only fused vertebrae are the four that comprise the sacrum and the vertebrae that compose your coccyx or tailbone. The coccyx is usually referred to as a single bone, but it's actually several vertebrae fused together. Tailbones are usually made of four fused vertebrae, but they can have anywhere from three to five.

The Head

The skull rests on the cervical part of the vertebral column, specifically on the first cervical vertebra, also known as the atlas. To allow energy to freely pass through the head, you need to begin by softening the muscles on the front and back of your neck, and imagine creating space between the seven cervical vertebrae of your neck. When we tense the muscles of the neck, especially the external muscles, like the sternocleidomastoid muscle, we prevent

Anabella teaching at Peridance Center, NYC, 2018

energy from flowing freely to the head, especially from the fontanel (where two sutures join in an infant to form a membrane-covered "soft spot"). When I explain to my students how to understand head alignment, I give them the following image to visualize: When standing up, imagine you are hanging from the top of your head (from the fontanel) like a Christmas ornament. Though your chin will feel tilted downward a bit, it is important for your eyes to remain open and look at the horizon, to obtain the neutral cervical curve.

Sometimes a choreographer will ask you to change your focus in a particular way. Doing so will affect the position and alignment of your head and neck, as well as your balance. Remember that the head is the heaviest part of your body! How you position your head will determine how gravity affects your movements. (See pages 84-85 for more on Gravity.)

The muscles of your face and neck must be relaxed as much as possible to allow the passage of energy through to the top of the head. Consider how the energy of your face passes through your skin into space and communicates with the audience. Sometimes I tell a performer to imagine that their head is like a light bulb, emanating light and energy outward. Sometimes I will make them imagine that the entire face is glowing in the dark!

When energy passes through the top of the head, the sensation is one of the whole crown lifting from the head, or that the volume of the head is as light as a balloon. I make my students aware of their fontanels. Other cultures, like the Sioux Native Americans, believe that when someone dies, their spirit exits through the holes of the body: (mouth, nose, ears, etc.) and also through the top of the head. The belief is that the top of the head has a connection to another dimension. Across all techniques, we need to feel this opening of the head when we dance.

When I work with actors and train their voices and resonators, for example, I make them visualize projecting the voice through the top of the head in a way that sends the sound up and out, expanding through the universe. In yoga, the fontanel is called the Sahasrara, or crown chakra, the highest chakra that sits at the crown of the head. The crown chakra represents our ability to be fully spiritually connected.

SKULL OF A NEWBORN

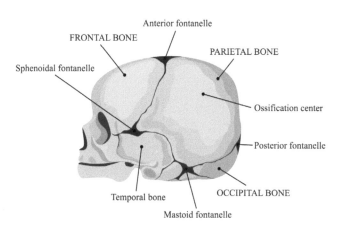

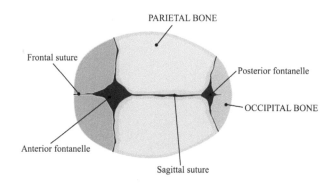

In a way, it's as if the top of the head is the top of an axis, what we call the axis mundi, between energy that is above us and energy that is below us. The fact that we remain upright and vertical is a statement that we are alive.

The Coccyx

The coccyx or tailbone anatomically points inward, not straight down. Many dance teachers state that the coccyx should point down or outward like a kangaroo tail. This imagery can help, but it's not anatomically correct. It's important to cross-check what you hear and deeply investigate what you are taught. For certain things, we need to use imagery to help us achieve something unrealistic, but that's not always the case.

The coccyx exists in relationship to the atlas, or first cervical vertebra, which articulates with the head.

Organizing Different Parts of the Spine

If you look at a skeleton, it's fascinating to explore where bones connect, how they connect, where small muscles and tendons insert, and how all of those things are connected together. This is why ever since I started teaching I've always brought a skeleton or anatomical drawings to class to help students understand the biomechanics of their bodies. I prefer to bring a skeleton rather than drawings because observing the skeleton in three dimensions helps students make deeper connections between action and anatomy.

When we begin to move certain parts of the body out of vertical alignment, how do we continue to feel the spine as the center of movement? If one of your legs moves out and up in grand-battement, how do you feel the standing leg is a continuation of the spine while at the same time isolating and elevating one part of the body? What is happening? The energy still flows in a vertical line from the top of your head to the standing leg, and the other leg moves in another direction. Moving one leg does not mean you forget you have a spine. This verticality of the spine will always be there when we are working standing up. With more contemporary floor work, how you visualize is different because you are horizontal or in another non-vertical position. I have noticed that many people are concerned about moving an arm, a leg, the head, etc., but forget about the unity of the body.

Left: Anabella explains the separation of the seven cervical vertebrae. Lauren Ohmer, dancer, 2015
Right: Anabella teaching at Peridance Center, NYC, 2018

As I tell my students, we are not like Frankenstein's monsters made of separate body parts from different people. Rather, we are one unified body that can isolate different body parts. Your spine connects all parts of your body, even though the center of movement differs according to technique. The spine is the "organizer" of the body's movement. Analyze the spinal position and you will understand a movement.

Isolation is a response to the center of movement and may affect your center of gravity, particularly how the energy passes through the entire body. It's hard to understand all of this information all at once while you are training, so it's important to take classes with the same teacher for quite some time to progressively understand the different methodologies of teaching and their specific didactics.

Discipline and consciousness take years to develop. We live in a culture where everything happens so quickly that we feel pressure to understand and assimilate the principles of movement as fast as possible, but it's simply not possible. The process is more important than the results! The results are a product of deep research.

The mind is sometimes quicker than the body, and sometimes the body is quicker than the mind. We must organize the entirety of the body in harmony: the physical body, the mind, the spirit, and energy.

As performers and teachers, an important concept is to understand your body through physically touching it. If you do not touch your body you do not know who you are, how heavy, soft, stiff, or blocked you are. Touch makes the body tangible. You need to know how tense you are, where muscles insert, where it hurts to the touch, what it feels like to touch tendons, what the articulation of your joints feels like, and so much more. Touch and manipulation of the body are fundamental to learning and teaching dance.

Here are some interesting facts about the spine:

- You have 33 bones in your spine.
- You need a healthy balance of muscle action to support proper body alignment.
- Your spine is capable of flexion, extension, side-bending, rotation, and all of these motions combined.
- Your intervertebral discs cushion curves in your vertebrae. Four curves in your spine act like springs on a mattress: two concave and two convex.
- Remember! While executing different dance movements, work on axial elongation, not muscular compression. Imagine creating more space between your vertebrae, like pearls on a necklace made of an elastic band.

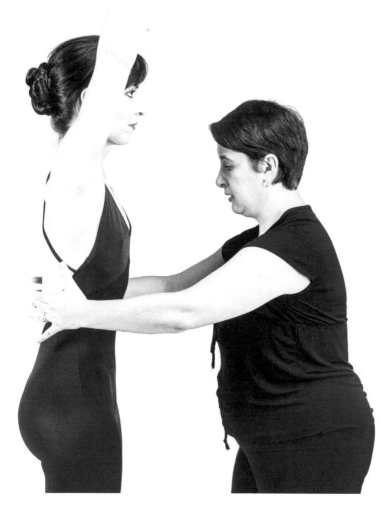

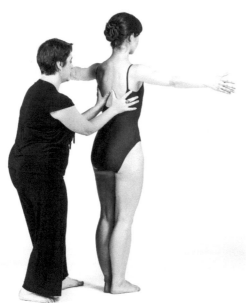

Top: Anabella explains the back & side expansion of the rib cage while breathing. Lauren Ohmer, dancer, 2015
Bottom: Anabella explains the back & side expansion of the rib cage while breathing. Lauren Ohmer, dancer, 2015

Rib Cage

Let us keep working down the body. We've reviewed the spine, so now let's look at the rib cage. Your rib cage is assembled from three types of bone—your sternum, 12 pairs of ribs, and 12 thoracic vertebrae. All of your ribs attach to your spine, but only the top seven pairs (known as "true ribs") connect to your sternum by strips of cartilage. The rib cage protects our organs, including the heart and lungs. Its other functions include assisting in respiration and providing support for the body's upper organs.

What is the alignment of the rib cage? Many times in the dance studio you will hear a teacher correcting students: "Please close your ribs" or "Don't push your ribs down so much," but what does this mean? Anatomically, these phrases are incorrect, but we can understand the intent. Teachers are often in a hurry to correct and fix a technical component. We need to solve problems quickly, and we sometimes are not as precise with our vocabulary as we could be. That's why we need to think and research outside of class!

As we know, you cannot open or close the rib cage. Internal and external muscles help to enlarge the capacity of the rib cage to expand the lungs, but the imagery of "opening" the ribs gives students the wrong impression. It's more helpful to work with the concept of "enlarging" or "expanding" the rib cage. I like to teach my students that to correctly align the ribs, the focus is not on the ribs themselves. Instead, the alignment or posture of the ribs is rooted in the spine because the ribs are all connected to the spine. Rather than saying "Close your ribs," I say, "Think of your spine alignment—the neutral spine—and imagine that when you breathe you expand your rib cage in three dimensions: side to side (X axis); upward and downward (Y axis); and forward and backward (Z axis). The rib cage hangs from the spine, so if the spine is in the right alignment (you feel your skeleton "hanging" from the fontanel), you will be able to breathe freely, and the rib cage will be in the right placement.

Once again imagine the whole spine as a necklace made of pearls (your vertebrae) on an elastic band. When you pull the elastic, the pearls separate to allow mobility between them. In this way, we can feel the rib cage floating, and we can expand our breath in three dimensions without relying only on shallow clavicular breathing from the top lobes of the lungs. We must focus on relaxing the chest, shoulders, and upper trapezius muscles at the bottom of your neck. You must direct your attention to the sensation of expanding the back of your ribs, where your lungs are positioned. You will feel "wings" open behind your ribs, like those of an angel. Imagine light emanating from the intercostal muscles that run between your ribs. Always keep in mind the image of "hanging" from the fontanel like a Christmas ornament.

This imagery is meant to help you to feel light. You may also feel a little "forward" in your alignment, but don't worry. Just make sure that you have the right weight distribution in the triangle delineated by the heel bone and the 1st and 5th toe. (Please see Feet & Ankles on page 131.)

To master this new sensation of lightness in your body, you must practice. It will not be enough to read about this imagery or listen to your teacher. The intellectual and creative parts of you must be expressed physically in order to be embodied. Take special care to first practice executing phrases of movement *in place*, without moving *across* space. When you feel you have mastered this, then practice the phrases while walking, then running, then leaping across the space. You will feel lighter, and it will be easier to defy gravity. Your lungs act like air bags or helium balloons, making the body lighter!

Rib cage

Anterior view

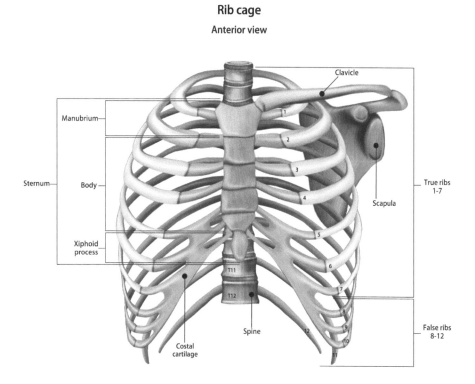

When I explain this concept to little kids, I sometimes use another image that I find helpful. I say, "Imagine that you have a crystal rose or a bird inside your rib cage. If you open the ribs too widely in the front, the rose will fall out or the bird will fly away. If you squeeze down on your ribs too much, you will squeeze the fragile rose or kill the bird." You want to create volume and space inside the rib cage, which allows the ribs to expand freely—sideways, vertically, and forward/backward. Always feel the connection of the rib cage to the spine.

I also imagine that the rib cage is like a set of blinds. Just as light passes through gaps between the blinds, we can imagine that our breath passes through the gaps between our ribs. Always think about expansion of the rib cage to the back and how your ribs are connected to the sternum in the front. Having a skeleton or a drawing of the rib cage at hand will help you grasp the shape of the ribs and more quickly assimilate technical elements.

At the front of the rib cage, over the sternum, we have the heart chakra. Don't forget to "open the energy" of this area, but remember to do so without lifting your shoulders and tensing your upper trapezius muscle.

In many techniques, including the Isadora Duncan technique, the heart chakra is the center of movement. When you see a dancer perform, you usually see the sternum shining like a beautiful pendant on a necklace. Dancers often lock all of their energy there. How will they convey emotions to the audience? We need to make the chest transparent by relaxing the ribs—especially the connection between the ribs and the sternum and clavicles—and allow the intercostal muscles to move freely.

Sometimes in daily life, we feel pressure in this heart chakra area—when we are sad, tense, stressed, or anxious. By opening up the heart chakra and allowing it to be an open door and open channel for emotions to pass, we are able to locate the emotional plane of existence as

103

dancers. I remember seeing Mikhail Baryshnikov perform live, and just seeing him walk on stage or take a bow, it was a revelation to see all of his heart chakra open and glowing. As a performer, you want to be a mirror for the audience. We need to relax our heart chakra, allow it to be free and open, and exchange energy and an emotional relationship with the audience. **Remember that performance is about generosity and about giving yourself.** Perhaps counterintuitively, it's also about being vulnerable, so how can we achieve that if our heart chakra is blocked?

I often recommend an exercise called "lateral breathing." It focuses on the even and symmetric expansion of the rib cage while breathing with awareness. You can do this exercise standing or sitting. Take a resistance band and wrap it around your ribs from the back and cross it in the front, holding the ends of the band with both hands. Start breathing, expanding your rib cage as much as you can, and feel the resistance band stretching. Using your hands, tighten the resistance band as you exhale. Focus on deep breathing, and repeat 5 times without hyperventilating. This is a good exercise to do every day before you start your daily training!

Facts about the rib cage:

- Small joints between the ribs and the vertebrae permit a gliding motion of the ribs on the vertebrae during breathing and other activities.
- The human skeleton has 12 pairs of ribs. Working from the top of the torso down, ribs 1 to 7 are considered "true ribs," as they connect directly from the spine to the sternum. Ribs 8 to 10 are called "false ribs" because they don't connect directly to the sternum, but have cartilage that attaches them to the sternum. Ribs 11 and 12 are called "floating ribs" because they only connect to the spine, not the sternum.
- The ribs are also called the thoracic cage.
- The muscles that connect to the ribs, the intercostal muscles (internal and external), and the diaphragm aid in breathing by expanding and contracting the rib cage. The serratus anterior; pectoralis major and minor; latissimus dorsi; scalenus anterior, posterior, and medius; and rectus abdominis are connected to the rib cage to support a stable upper body.

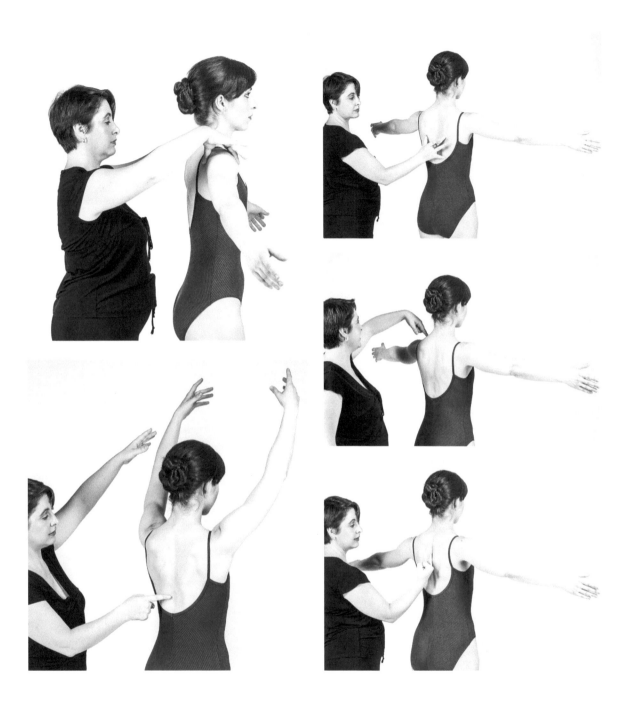

Top Left and Right: Anabella explains how to separate the scapula using the rhomboid muscles while holding a port de bras. Lauren Ohmer, dancer, 2015

Bottom Left: Anabella explains the engagement of the dorsal muscles while holding a port de bras. Lauren Ohmer, dancer, 2015

Middle Right: Anabella explains the relaxation of the upper trapezius muscles while holding a port de bras. Lauren Ohmer, dancer, 2015

Bottom Right: Anabella explains how to retract the scapula using the rhomboid muscles while holding a port de bras. Lauren Ohmer, dancer, 2015

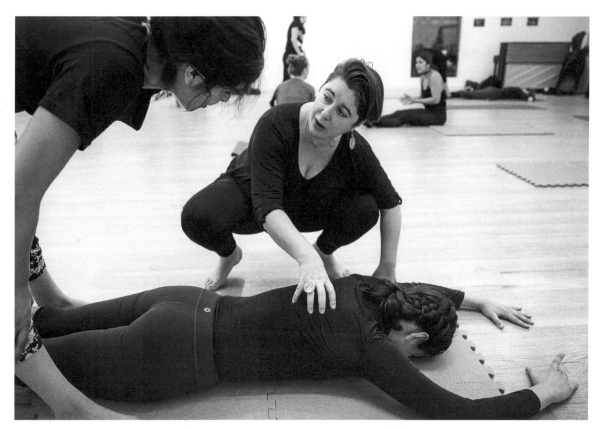

Top: Anabella explains the separation of the scapula at Peridance Center, NYC, 2018
Bottom: Anabella teaching the flow of energy through the arms at Peridance Center, NYC, 2018

Shoulders & Arms

Let us move now to the back of the rib cage and the gliding joint of the scapulae. The scapulae are flat triangular bones commonly called shoulder blades. A scapula is one of three bones that forms each shoulder joint. They connect your clavicle (collarbone) to your humerus (upper arm bones).

The scapula is an important bone in the function of the shoulder joint. It engages in six types of motion that allow for full-functional upper-extremity movement, including elevation and depression. They are commonly described as translatory motions in which the scapula moves upward or downward along the rib cage from its resting position. These motions are protraction and retraction, upward and downward rotation, internal/external rotation, and anterior/posterior tipping.

Our shoulder blades slide back and forth along the back of the rib cage and allow for the movement of the arms. Each person's body structure is different, so each person's shoulder blades will look different. On some people it looks like the shoulder blades are sticking out like little wings. Some people naturally have less protruding or flat-appearing shoulder blades. Some people have shoulder blades that are placed closer to one another on either side of the spine, whereas other people may have shoulder blades that appear farther apart.

Regardless of body structure, all dancers must aim to achieve stability of the scapulae and to anchor them downward. Being aware of the distance between each scapula and the spine is important. The muscles that are placed diagonally between the scapulae and spine are rhomboid minor (superior) and rhomboid major.

It can help to ask another dancer to put their hands over your shoulder blades and to feel the different movements in your body in order for you to understand how the scapulae glide over your ribs.

Another exercise is to retract your shoulder blades together closer to the spine, as if you want to hold something between them. Then separate them without contracting the muscles of your chest or rounding your back. You can do this lying down on your back on the floor or from a standing position.

Creating space between your shoulder blades allows thoracic or dorsal vertebrae to spread energy from the spine through to the arm. Remember the relationship between the fourth dorsal (L4) vertebra and the arms that I discussed in the section First Alignment, Then Movement starting on page 94. If the shoulder blades are squeezed together in a natural fashion and there is considerable tension, your energy will not be able to pass from the T4 vertebra to the arms. The pathway of energy goes from T4 to scapula to tricep muscles to elbow to the muscle on the back of the forearm, and then to the middle finger! Yes, the special middle finger in your hand.

My dance training in *braceo* (movement of the arms) in flamenco and in *port de bras* in ballet shared this same line of energy projection from T4 all the way to the middle finger. I remember my flamenco teacher saying "move the hands once in an inward circle and once outwards. The initiation of the movement is the middle finger!" And now you can see it is no coincidence that my ballet teacher said: "When you do a *grand plie* and the *port de bras* is accompanied by *en dehors*, think about the resistance of the middle finger in the air, like it's pushing something, so you can connect your arms with your back muscles!"

This is the way to feel the dorsal muscles on your back engaging and anchoring your arms to your trunk. Practicing *barre à terre*—especially lying on your back and working on your *port de bras*—will make you aware of all the muscles that you forget you're using while you are dancing standing up.

One good exercise to practice this opening action is as follows:

1. Lie on the floor on your back with your arms perpendicular to the spine that is flat on the floor. Your palms should face the ceiling.
2. Squeeze your shoulder blades together, imagining that you're trying to hold a pencil between your shoulder blades.
3. Now spread your shoulder blades out to the sides without tensing the muscles around your clavicle or closing the heart chakra. Feel the opening action that allows energy to pass freely from your dorsal vertebrae to your shoulder blades, into the arms, and then into the middle fingers, projecting to infinity.

Some people, like me, have a body structure in which the shoulders naturally drape forward. It is important to be aware of this tendency if this is your body structure. You must also be aware of what it feels like when your shoulders drape backward too far. You must find what it feels like to be right in the center. Imagine that your collar bone is a hanger off which the arms and rib cage hang when they are relaxed.

Caution! When we lack awareness of the muscles that anchor the scapulae, or if they are weak, we sometimes use our sternomastoid muscles in the front of our necks and our upper trapezius muscles that extend across the tops of our shoulders to hold up our arms and our collar bones. This causes us to tense up and look like Arnold Schwarzenegger! I recommend avoiding this at all cost! Instead, imagine creating more space between your ears and your shoulders, elongating your neck and seven cervical vertebrae. Open your heart chakra and anchor your scapulae!

Facts about the shoulders and scapulae:

- Scapulae can vary in size and shape between individuals.
- Scapulae are crucial bones that support shoulder movement and stability.
- Proper scapula positioning and movement are essential for good posture and pain-free shoulder functionality.
- The scapula acts as a site for muscle and ligament attachments.
- The scapula is responsible for the shoulder's wide range of motion.
- The scapula is susceptible to muscle imbalances and postural issues.
- Weakness or tightness in certain muscles can lead to issues like rounded shoulders or shoulder impingement.
- A total of 17 muscles attach to the scapulae.

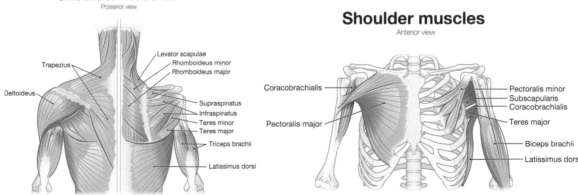

Arms & Hands

The spine exists in relation to the shoulder blades and thus the bones of the arm: the humerus in the upper arm and the radius and ulna in the forearm. The radius connects to the thumb. I call it your "antenna." When you move the arm to the side, you must not block energy flow through the elbow articulation by hyperextending the elbow joint. Allow energy to pass freely from the T4 vertebra to the middle finger, projecting into space. I remember my Humphrey/Limón teachers telling me, "The elbow is like a thermometer of the emotions. If you tense your elbows, the hand and the rest of the arms are lifeless!"

When you have to give a child a bath and you test the temperature of the water before allowing the kid to jump in, you should test it with your elbow. Why? Because it allows nervous and energetic information to pass through the arm to the spinal cord, or the center of the nervous system, which then tells your brain whether the water is too hot. Many people hyperextend their elbows or bend their arms, blocking energy flow to one of the most expressive parts of the body, the hands. It is also important not to block energy at the wrist.

The middle finger is very interesting. In modern dance, flamenco, Hindu dances, and yoga, the middle finger is very powerful. In ballet we use resistance from the middle finger to push or cut the air in turns, penché, promenade, etc. Remember: The middle finger is connected with the spine. You will move your hands in different ways according to a specific aesthetic or style, but it is always the middle finger that initiates the movement unless the choreographer you're working with is exploring another source of initiation to investigate a different aesthetic or body sensation. Also, depending on the style or technique of performance, other fingers may also carry different expressions, like the mudras in eastern dances. If you follow the line of energy from the middle finger toward the center of the body, you'll see that it comes from the spine. When we see that someone's middle finger is connected energetically to the rest of their body, we can notice how they project their energy.

The hands and face are the most expressive parts of the body and are how we relate to the world. Hands are an extension of our minds. They express intellectual information. Our faces express emotional information. Together, hands and face make up a large part of our body's expression.

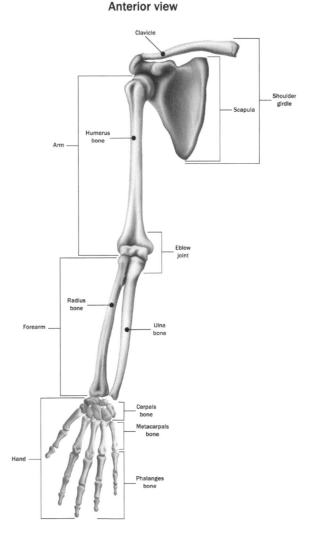

Bones of the upper limb

Anterior view

Clavicle

Shoulder girdle

Scapula

Humerus bone

Arm

Eblow joint

Radius bone

Ulna bone

Forearm

Carpals bone

Metacarpals bone

Hand

Phalanges bone

Top Left: Anabella shows dancers how to stretch the muscles of the wrist using your fingers (part 1) at Peridance Center, NYC, 2018
Bottom Left: Anabella shows dancers how to stretch the muscles of the wrist using your fingers (part 2), feeling the palm of the hand in order to project energy, Peridance Center, NYC, 2018
Top Right: Anabella teaching the projection of energy through the middle fingers, Peridance Center, NYC, 2018
Bottom Right: Anabella teaching projection of energy through the palms of the hands and fingers, Heifetz Institute, VA, 2023

Whether on the floor or standing up, we must move while thinking about the center of energy in the spine, head, ribs, pelvis, and legs. Relax your muscles. Also feel the relationship between the hands and the shoulder blades to the spine.

Facts about the arms and hands:

- Each arm of the human body has 30 bones. It has one humerus (upper arm), one ulna and one radius (forearm), eight carpals (wrist bones), five metacarpals (palm bones), and 14 phalanges (five digits).
- The human arm has a remarkable range of motion, thanks to its intricate joint structure.
- The arm muscles, particularly the biceps and triceps, are among the strongest muscles in the body.
- Our hands have 27 bones, 123 ligaments, 34 muscles, 48 nerves, and 30 arteries.
- There are no actual muscles located in your fingers and thumbs. Instead, your digits move by the action of almost 40 muscles located in your forearm and hand. The tendons of these muscles run into the fingers and attach to the bone to move your fingers, much like a rope and pulley system.
- About a quarter of the motor cortex in the human brain (the part of the brain which controls all movement in the body) is devoted to the muscles of the hands.

Hips, Pelvis & Core

The pelvis functions as the reservoir for the abdominal organs, including the bladder, intestines, and uterus in women or prostate in men.

The pelvis is a symmetrical bony girdle and is composed of three strong bones fused together: the *ilium, ischium,* and *pubis*. These bones merge to form bilateral concave sockets named *acetabulum,* which accommodate the femur heads to form the hip joints, major ball-and-socket joints connecting the femur to the pelvis.

The *ilium* is the largest flat bone located on either side of the upper portion of the pelvis, including the *iliac crest,* which is the protruding tip bone of the pelvis (see images on page 112).

The *pubis* is the smallest bone on the anterior side of the pelvis. Both ends of the pelvis are fused by the *symphysis pubis,* consisting of cartilaginous flexible tissue.

Males and females differ significantly in the anatomy of the pelvis: A female *pelvis* is wider and the *pubis* shorter than a male's. This is an anatomical adaptation to child-bearing and birth. In pregnant women the *symphysis* is extended to allow for the passage of the child through the birth canal.

Many ligaments, tendons, and muscles are attached to the femur and hip sockets or *acetabulum.* Reviewing an image of a skeleton can be a great way to understand the shape and volume of the hips. I also highly recommend that students use touch to explore their own bodies to understand the shape of the pelvis and compare it to the 3D skeleton in class.

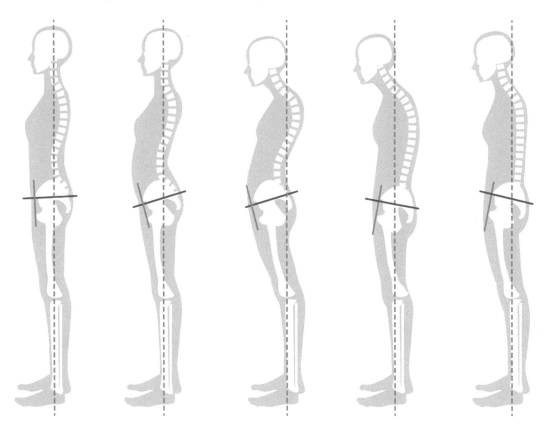

Relationship between the plumb line and the placement of the pelvis to obtain a neutral spine alignment.

The placement of the pelvis in dance is fundamental in maintaining the neutral spine, mastering balance, and moving the legs properly and freely. I like to imagine that the pelvis is like a glass of wine. If you tip this glass forward and your pubic bone passes the middle line of the body, the wine will pour out. Doing this will interrupt the flow of energy in the lumbar spine, sacrum, and coccyx, and it will disconnect the spine from the legs. Incorrect positioning of the pelvis will alter the natural connection between the head and the center of gravity, making it counterproductive.

Please do not tense the gluteus maximus and quadriceps! One risk is commonly called "taking the pelvis," a phrase that encapsulates a complex issue. You want to avoid overusing your gluteus maximus, which will block the natural function of the six rotator muscles, overstretch your psoas muscle (which is deep in your core), crunch your pectineus muscle in your thigh, and overwork your quadriceps. It will limit the freedom of your entire pelvis, hips, and lower spine! See the images that illustrate this issue on page 111.

How to Find the Right Placement of Your Pelvis

We need to find the right placement of the pelvis, which depends on the shape of your pelvis. Concentrate on relaxing the gluteus maximus and visualizing the sacrum ilium joint. Engage the four layers of your abdominals, and lengthen the back erector muscles. Focus on your verticality and feel your spine lengthening. Imagine that the pubic bone and coccyx are like two pendulums pointing down to the earth. It is important to feel the shape, dimensions, and weight of your pelvis to move in space.

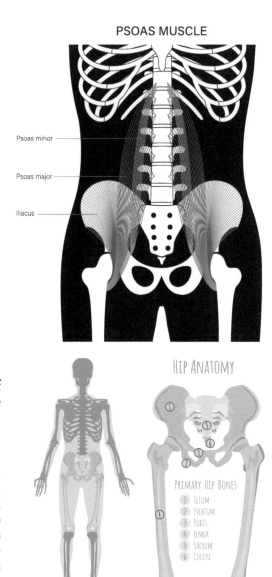

The placement of the hip should not be thought of as a visual effect but, rather, as a body mechanic, a necessity for mastering your art of performance.

Why do many people experience so much difficulty in allowing the muscles around the hips to relax? The gluteus maximus muscles usually overpower the rest of the muscles that surround the hips because they are naturally quite strong. If your core muscles are weak, then you rely on the gluteus maximus and quadriceps to help you. The body senses weakness, calls 911, and the gluteus maximus shows up in a hurry to solve technical difficulties while you dance.

In my classes, I always talk about the notion that we have "four layers of muscles" in the human body from the outermost to the innermost. When we are in "emergency" and our inner-layer muscles are weak, we tend to overuse the superficial outer muscles.

When I teach technique and explain muscle work, I always bring with me the book *Albinus on Anatomy*. This beautiful book represents the rarest of human achievements: a work of great scientific merit that is a magnificent work of art as well. Bernard Siegfried Albinus (1697-1770) was the greatest descriptive anatomist of the 18th century. His book includes drawings of bones and muscles from different vantage points, from the outermost order of muscles to the second, third, and fourth orders.

The muscles of the back can be divided into three groups—superficial, intermediate, and intrinsic or deep.

- Superficial muscles are associated with movements of the shoulder.
- Intermediate muscles are associated with movements of the thoracic cage.
- Intrinsic or deep muscles are associated with movements of the vertebral column island and help tremendously in the carriage of our arms.
- I use this anatomical information in class to help students understand the complexities of the human body. Being aware of each muscle group's specificity allows us to analyze, discern, and specify our movements.

Whatever book you learn from and share with your students, make sure it has muscular details and artistic details. As dancers we must have muscular control to give us artistic choices. Art is about choice, not chance!

But let's come back to the pelvis: Tensing the gluteus muscles can become a habit, like biting your lips or tensing your jaw. Doing so accumulates tension and inhibits movement. The gluteus maximus is the largest and heaviest muscle in the body. It is also the most superficial of all gluteal muscles.

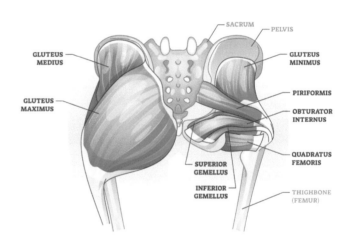

GLUTES

POSTERIOR VIEW

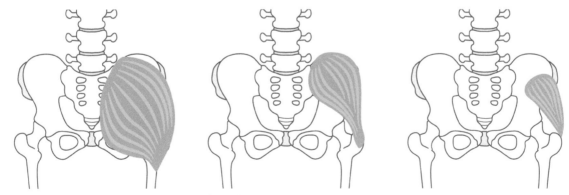

From left to right: Gluteus Maximus, Gluteus Medius, Gluteus Minimus

113

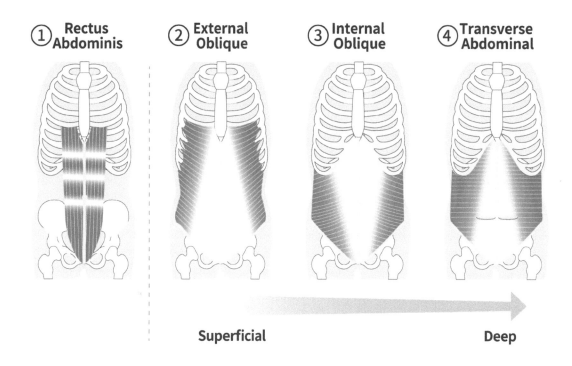

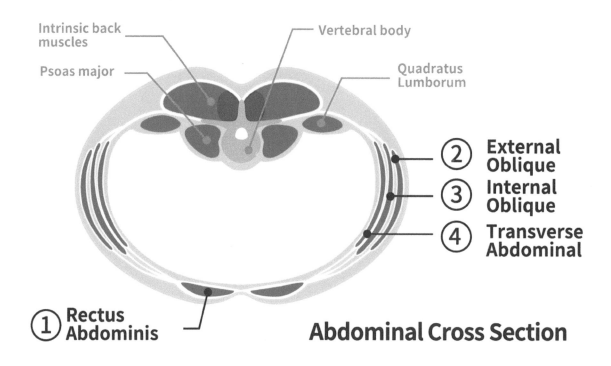

Intrinsic back muscles

Psoas major

Vertebral body

Quadratus Lumborum

② External Oblique

③ Internal Oblique

④ Transverse Abdominal

① Rectus Abdominis

Abdominal Cross Section

The functions of the gluteus maximus are the extension and external rotation of the thigh at the hip joint. Its superior part can produce thigh abduction (the movement of a limb away from the midline of the body), whereas the inferior part causes the thigh adduction (when you move a limb toward the center of the body).

To find a middle point at which the hip bone just hangs, we must relax the gluteus maximus and visualize the hip in relation to the spine. This allows the lower back to decompress and energy to flow up and down the spine.

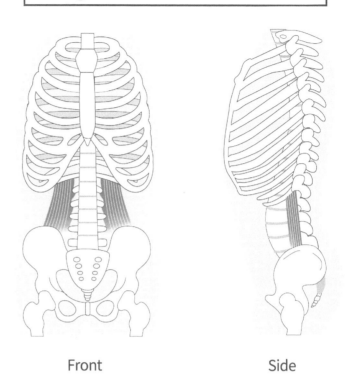

Quadratus Lumborum

Front   Side

We must also begin to think about the relationship between hips and ribs. We have five lumbar vertebrae between the two. Think of this relationship as a game of "Jenga" with bones. What is their relational position? We know that the rib cage hangs from the spine. Do the hips also hang from the spine? How does gravity affect the rib cage and hips? Let the sensation of your hanging rib cage and hips relax your muscles. Then feel the space between the rib cage and the front of your iliac crest, as well as the separation between the back of your ribs and your hips. It is here where the abdominal muscles play their important role.

What do we call the core? Your core musculature can be referred to in various ways: center, trunk, abdomen, power house, spine stabilizers, torso, and abdominal wall, but what muscles constitute the core musculature? The following muscles, when combined as a whole, make up the core:

- **Pelvic floor.** Sitting at the base of your core, the pelvic floor consists of the skeletal muscles that support the bladder and bowels, as well as women's reproductive organs.
- **Internal and external abdominal obliques.** Located above the pelvic floor, these two pairs of muscles stack up the sides of your core, allowing your trunk to twist and turn.
- **Transverse abdominis.** Set deep in the abdomen and wrapping around the spine, the transverse abdominis serves as the core's main stabilizer muscle by supporting spine and pelvis. It also protects and supports your internal organs.
- **Erector spinae.** This large, deep muscle helps straighten and rotate your back and also plays a role in stability. Erector spinae weakness can cause back pain.
- **Rectus abdominis.** Though the rectus abdominis are known as the "six pack" muscles, they are actually just two muscles separated vertically by the linea alba. Set between the transverse abdominis at the front of your abdomen, these muscles aid in core stability and movement.

The gluteus medius and minimus are also important to the stability of the pelvis. The quadratus lumborum, the deepest back muscles (big elastic bands that connect the back of the rib cage to the hips) also contribute to the stabilization and movement of the spine and the pelvis. A bilateral contraction of those muscles leads to an extension of the lumbar vertebral column. See the images on page 113.

Now, let's talk about some rather old-fashioned instructions that dance teachers unfortunately still sometimes give: "Tummy in!" and "Squeeze the glutes!" We can do better than that! After all, how can you dance when you are really pulling your stomach in? Doing so creates tension and immobility and also prevents you from breathing deeply. Rather than creating meaningful movement with strong technique, all too often this advice leads a dancer to block themselves and their potential. You must remember that the words you give to students to describe technique are very important.

I strongly recommend studying anatomy and understanding muscle function!

Here are some images I share with my students as they work to engage their cores:

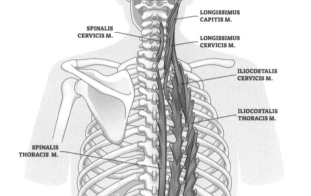

ERECTOR SPINAE MUSCLES

- Imagine you have a kimono belt (an *obi*) wrapped around your body between your ribs and hips. Your transversus abdominis runs horizontally like an *obi*. Do your best to engage it!
- Lift a zipper from your pubic bone to the bottom edge of your sternum. The fibers of the abdominal rectum run vertically, like the imaginary zipper.
- Lift the strap of your bikini, think about Jane Fonda's 1980 high-cut leotards, and lift the internal obliques, your sexy "V" muscles!
- "Hold your pee," when engaging your pelvic floor muscles.
- To explain the function of the erector spinae muscles and dorsals, I like to note that you do not dance from the front of your body. You dance from the back—from your spine— and you move your spine in space when you dance. Imagine your ancestors pushing you from behind! Feel the energy coming from the back and passing like a wave, washing over and through you to the front.
- People are often nervous about placement of the pelvis. However, if you focus on your spine's alignment, your hips will automatically fall into place. In other words, if you relax your butt, you will be in place.

Each of us has a different body structure, training, and imagination. We need to work on how our body performs actions from the inside, not the outside, not on how we *think* an action should look. For example, some people will always look like they have a "tucked in" pelvis from the outside. You see people standing in line for the bus, at the bank, or supermarket, and you see that their hips are tilted backward. Daily posture influences dance posture!

On the other hand, when we dance, we work to achieve what we call our own natural, neutral position through which energy can flow freely.

Technique in performance and dance is having command of each part of the body, such as the placement of your pelvis, and being in command of your inner impulses.

Technique is being aware of the entire body as a medium of communication in time and space.

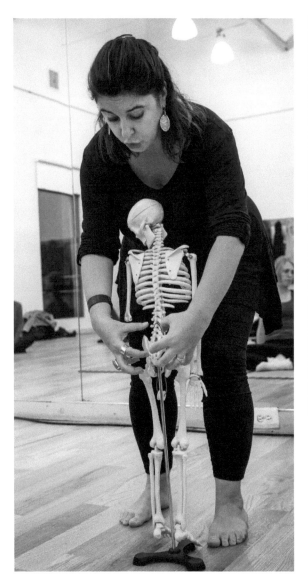

Left: Anabella explaining creation of space between the back of the ribs and the back of the hips using the quadratus lumborum at Peridance Center, NYC, 2020

Top Right: Anabella explaining creation of space in the sacroiliac joint while engaging the lower abdominals, Peridance Center, NYC, 2020

Bottom Right: Anabella explaining the creation of space in the hip joint while engaging the core, Peridance Center, NYC, 2018

All Images: Anabella teaching the engagement of the core, Peridance Center, NYC, 2018

Legs & Hips

The most expressive part of the body is the face, followed by the hands, then torso, arms, and feet, with the legs coming in last. Ballet technique has evolved over the past 400 years, but the function of the feet and legs in the beginning was simply to transport the dancer through space. Dancing itself was synonymous with transporting the body in space, creating shapes and patterns. Later, when Romanticism swept the dance world, pointe shoes appeared, and finally, with the arrival of the choreographer and teacher Marius Petipa and the creation of Classical ballet, leg movement became the symbol of virtuosity.

When we trace the development of dance costumes over time, we discover that pants and skirts gradually became shorter and shorter until they evolved into the classical tutu and, later, just tights, leotards, and unitards. Little by little, emphasis moved toward showcasing the legs.

In my life as a teacher I've seen many dancers from different disciplines and dance techniques seek to make their legs more "expressive" and "sexy," and legs are still the main protagonist in the story of ballet today. In the text that follows, I will try to cover as much ground as possible and summarize 35 years of teaching people how to be aware of their legs and feet.

Covering functional anatomy in this section has been one of the most complicated for me. I have much more to say on the topic, so you must come and take my classes if you want to go deeper! Sometimes words are not enough. Practical exercises are the best teachers. And here we go!

Parallel, Turn-in & Turnout Leg Positions

In any type of dance—from tango to flamenco, jazz, modern, and ballet—you need to master only three leg positions in order to dance: parallel, turn-in, and turnout (*en dehors*). In ballet we have seven positions, including the *en dehors* variations.

I always explain that the most important factor is understanding the position of the femur in the hip socket or acetabulum. The top part of the femur (see image on page 122) has two protruding extremities: the greater trochanter and the lesser trochanter. Take a minute to study the image closely and identify them in your body. It's important!

- The **greater trochanter** is the protruding extremity of the upper femur that can be felt laterally at the hip. The primary function of the greater trochanter is to serve as an attachment site for several muscles in the hip region. Notably, it provides attachments for muscles responsible for abducting and rotating the thigh, including parts of the gluteus medius and gluteus minimus muscles, as well as the piriformis, obturator internus, and superior and inferior gemelli. In addition, the greater trochanter serves as an attachment point for hip ligaments, which contribute to the stability and integrity of the hip joint.
- The **lesser trochanter** is a bony projection from the shaft of the femur. It serves as the principal insertion site of the *iliopsoas* muscle.

The greater trochanter is the key to understanding the three leg positions that must be mastered in order to dance. Locating and feeling the greater trochanter with your hands on your own body is fundamental.

First, in parallel position with feet and legs, rock your pelvis side to side, and you will feel the greater trochanter, like an indentation. You could also execute a *tendu à la seconde* in parallel and you will feel it. You may be asking, How do I properly stand in true parallel position?

The feet are separated by a distance of approximately one foot or wider, toes straight forward and parallel. The lines that are parallel are the lines made by the outside of your feet, not the insides or some imaginary line in the middle of each foot.

Next, in *en dehors* or turnout position (sometimes called outward position), place both hands on both trochanters while repeatedly activating and disengaging your six deep external rotator muscles. The six deep external rotator muscles of the hip (piriformis, quadratus femoris, obturator internus, obturator externus, superior gemellus, and inferior gemellus) play a role in hip stabilization and hip rotation. They are responsible for the rotation of the femur into the hip socket! You can never achieve a correct *en dehors* without engaging these muscles. However, they don't work alone. This group of six muscles and the adductor group of muscles work together. The principal actors are the six deep rotators, and the assistants are the adductors. (The hip adductors are five muscles located in the medial compartment of the thigh. They are the adductor longus, adductor brevis, adductor magnus, gracilis, and pectineus.)

There are several reasons why dancers use turnout:

- **Alignment.** Turnout helps to correctly align the body while dancing. By rotating the legs outward from the hips, dancers can achieve better alignment of knees, ankles, and feet, which is crucial for proper balance, stability, and aesthetics in dance movements.
- **Range of Motion and Balance.** Turnout increases the range of motion in the hips and allows dancers to execute movements like jumps, turns, and extensions more efficiently and with greater ease. It also helps with balance.
- **Aesthetics.** Turnout is considered aesthetically pleasing in many dance styles, as it creates long, clean lines and shapes with the body. It also enhances the overall grace and fluidity of movements, contributing to beauty and elegance.
- **Historical Tradition.** Turnout has been a fundamental aspect of classical ballet technique for centuries and is deeply rooted in the history and tradition of ballet. Turnout started in the early days of ballet as a way to present the feet and ankles in their best angles and to help dancers' range of motion and control of their balance. Turnout is particularly emphasized in ballet, but it is also used to varying degrees in other dance styles, such as modern dance, jazz, and contemporary dance. It's also used in folk and traditional dances around the world, such as classical Indian dances. However, the degree of turnout and its importance varies according to the specific dance style and technique being practiced.
- **Turn-In.** This position of the legs and feet is mostly used in some folk dances and jazz, where the feet and head of the femur are pointed inward.
- **Note:** Proper alignment means that the knee is *always* directly over the toes in all three leg positions in order to prevent injury to the hip, knee, and ankle!

In any of these positions we always must feel the trochanter's presence. It is hard for many to physically feel the round part of the head of the femur, so it might be helpful to visualize or internalize the trochanter as the origin of our legs' position to make your movements more fluid, more precise, and, yes, more expressive.

Once you have become aware of the sensation of the femur and trochanter as the origin of the movement of your leg, proceed to relaxing all the superficial muscles of the leg and the hip articulation so you can efficiently control the precise leg movement, particularly quick movement. Watch slow motion videos of elite Olympic runners, for example, and pay attention to their faces: They will be relaxed, without tension, because every ounce of energy is being poured into the exact muscles and fibers the runners need to win the race.

When we are in parallel, we should feel as if a skewer is passing from one side of the hip through to the other. We should feel that the two sides are connected. It is important that when you are in parallel you are truly in parallel—not half-way between parallel and turned out, or slightly turned in. Imagine that parallel position is like speaking English, and a turned out position is like speaking Spanish. Do not speak Spanglish. It is the in between that can be dangerous.

Being in parallel evokes a very specific feeling. Get to know this feeling. To find the appropriate position, get to know the lines created by the outside of your feet. Some people experience more or less rotation of the leg from the knee down, but what is important is the position of the femur's origin. Track the knee in the same line as the big toe.

In turnout, the femur rotates in the hip socket. This is where turnout comes from, not from rotating the knee. A common unhealthy practice is to rotate from the knee down or, perhaps worse, turning and sacrificing the ankle joint. You will end up with a twisted knee, not a turned out leg. To rotate the head of the femur, you must engage the six deep rotator muscles that you use to operate the movement of the head of the femur in the hip socket. The gluteus maximus cannot actively be involved in the turnout because if you engage and contract it, you actually prevent yourself from feeling the use and function of the six deep rotators! To reiterate: When you are turned out, you also feel your trochanters.

Some people think that the abductors' function in turnout is to squeeze the legs together (in fifth position, for example), but in reality their function is to rotate the femur in the hip socket while keeping the knee in alignment. Someone may initially appear to be in a fully turned out position, but on closer inspection a practiced eye can see they are using the gluteus maximus and tensing the IT band. It's distracting and, even worse, suggests poor training, insecurity, and that the dancer is not in full command of their body. Much of the choreographer's intention will not be expressed clearly, like a photograph that is out of focus. The stability of your standing leg comes from rotating the femur in the hip socket and engaging the six deep rotators and the adductors.

Note: The act of turning out is a continuous action, not a static position. The energy of rotation never stops. Turning out is an ongoing movement.

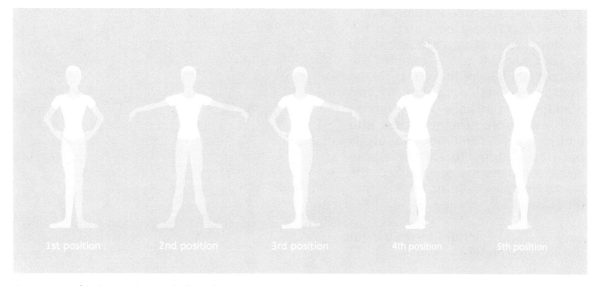

Five positions of the legs and arms in ballet technique

Identifying the Leg Muscles

What are the names of the muscle groups that surround your legs? Why do we need to know their function? Simply put, we cannot master the use of the legs if we don't know everything about them. In my classes I always say, "Your legs aren't made of sausage!" Knowing about each muscle and its function helps you achieve more control. As the American choreographer and teacher Anna Halprin said, "The mind informs the body and the body informs the mind."

The muscles in your legs are: quadriceps, hamstrings, adductors, and the iliotibial (IT) band. Let's get to know them!

Quadriceps

The quadriceps are a group of muscles present on the front of the thigh. They consist of four distinct muscles: the rectus femoris, the vastus lateralis, the vastus intermedius, and the vastus medialis. The function of the quadriceps is to extend the leg at the knee joint and flex the thigh at the hip joint. They also help stabilize the knee by holding the patella inside a groove in the femur, or thigh bone. The quadricep muscles work antagonistically with the hamstring muscles. When one muscle group contracts, the other relaxes, allowing for flexion and extension of the knee.

Hamstrings

The hamstring muscles are three large muscles that run down the back of the thigh and help control the hips and knees—the biceps femoris, semitendinosus, and semimembranosus. Their function is to extend (open) the hip joint, increasing the angle between your pelvis and thigh; flex (bend) your knee; and rotate the leg at the hip and knee joints.

Adductors

The muscles in the medial compartment of the thigh are collectively known as the hip adductors. There are four primary muscles in this group: adductor longus, adductor brevis, adductor magnus, and gracilis. These muscles' primarily function is to move the thigh/lower extremity closer to the body's central axis.

Iliotibial Band

The iliotibial (IT) band is a long fibrous piece of fascia tissue that runs from the outside of your hip down to the outside of your knee. It has a complex job description: It helps lift your leg to the front and to the side of your body, and it supports your knee during flexion and extension. The muscles into which the IT band attaches at its proximal end, the tensor fascia latae and the gluteus maximus, affect the amount of shortness or tension that the IT band has.

Look at the images and identify them in your own body!

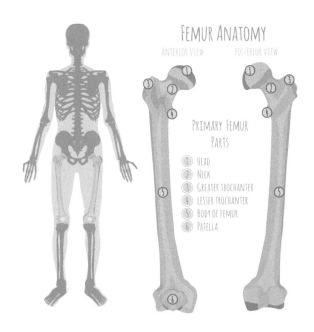

FEMUR ANATOMY

ANTERIOR VIEW   POSTERIOR VIEW

PRIMARY FEMUR PARTS

1. HEAD
2. NECK
3. GREATER TROCHANTER
4. LESSER TROCHANTER
5. BODY OF FEMUR
6. PATELLA

Hip & Leg Muscles & Dance

Our hips and legs help us keep connected to the earth using weight. The weight of your hips and legs, acting with gravity in downward movements, counterbalances the lightness of the torso extending upward.

Remember that knowledge of anatomy informs how we think about and practice our range of movement, among other things! We know that the range of movement of our legs is circular because the hip is a ball-and-socket joint, for example. When the femur is not in an aligned position and you don't respect your neutral spine, your femur lacks the space in the starting position necessary to rotate into the hip socket using the proper muscles. Think of your six deep rotators and your adductors as brakes on a bicycle: They stabilize the femur into the hip socket.

Quadriceps & Knees

Let's also talk about the quadriceps. When you turn out by using the six deep rotators and your adductors, you are not involving your quadriceps or gluteus maximus.

The adductors exist in relation to the heels. Between the two, of course, we have the knees. How do we feel about this relationship, and what do we do with the knees? Some teachers say you need to "lift" your knees. However, when you lift the knees, you actually engage the quadriceps, and—depending on the shape of the legs in question—you can sometimes hyperextend the knees and completely block the

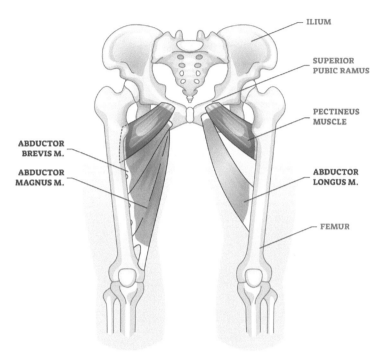

PECTINEUS

ILIUM

SUPERIOR PUBIC RAMUS

PECTINEUS MUSCLE

ABDUCTOR LONGUS M.

FEMUR

ABDUCTOR BREVIS M.

ABDUCTOR MAGNUS M.

ANTERIOR VIEW

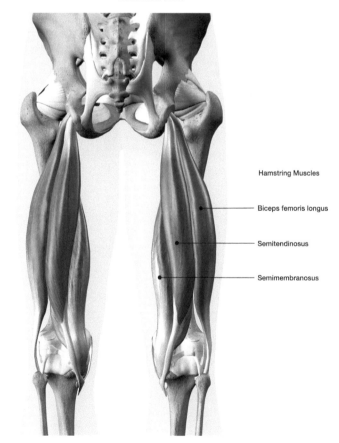

Hamstring Muscles

Biceps femoris longus

Semitendinosus

Semimembranosus

knee joint. I therefore suggest that teachers change the lexicon and say something like "Lift from the inside of your legs like a zipper," providing the image of the active adductors and relaxed quadriceps. This particular example would be best for a dancer in a fixed first or fifth position in ballet.

If you wrap a flexible rubber band, like a TheraBand, around the heel and extend its length along the inside line of your leg to where the abductor inserts in the pubic bone, you will feel the opposition of the heel pressing down and the abductors rotating up as you move into a turned out position. You will feel the entire internal part of the leg working. The quadriceps should remain about 90% relaxed because the proper function of the quadriceps is not to rotate the legs in a static position.

When you elevate your leg 90 degrees in front, you are using your quadriceps to elevate the legs, but the deep six rotators (the adductors) actually rotate the leg. When you elevate your legs, it's like your body has two teams working together to make that action happen. One team extends and the other team contracts: Hamstrings do an extrinsic contraction and quadriceps an intrinsic contraction. If you overwork your quadriceps to lift your legs in turned out position, you develop excess tension and the legs feel incredibly

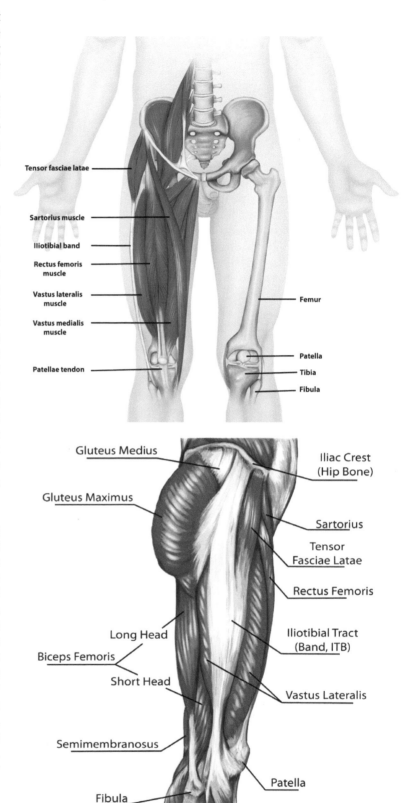

heavy. Practice your control of muscle activation. **Notice and encourage relaxation of the muscles that are unnecessary.**

More on Turnout

When you are in turned out positions it is very important that you feel the internal line of the legs. The common advice given when practicing turnout is to make sure the knees are directly over the big toes. This is helpful, to be sure, but it is not the first chapter in the turnout story! Good turnout is the secondary effect of the six deep rotators and adductors rotating the femur. If you start by thinking "knees over toes," you're likely to use your quadriceps to achieve the position. If you begin by thinking of abductors rotating your femurs in the hip sockets, you'll find your knees will automatically follow the line of your toes. It's simple for me to write and say when I'm teaching class. When you incorporate and feel the difference, you will immediately understand that technique feeds artistry.

Motion creates emotion, and emotion creates motion.

Let us turn now to the standing leg *en dehors*: Remember that in turned out positions, you should always feel the relationship among the heel, abductor, and trochanter, as well as the action of the six rotator muscles. This sensation is especially necessary for your standing leg—when executing a *rond de jambe en dehors* from first position in ballet, for example. The muscle engagement and consciousness stabilizes you. I always say, **"The standing leg is the continuation of the spine, energetically speaking."** We must feel energy traveling from the top of the head through the spine, through the sit bones all the way to the heel bone.

Legs & Dance

When you dance, your legs must feel as light as feathers! This is almost always the goal—unless your choreographer/director instructs you to move with legs that feel like heavy potato bags! Technique is technique. It is a foundation. Many great works of art in all media have been made with nothing more than good technique. In dance, technique trains the body to work toward lightness, creating easy fluid movement. If the choreographer wants to do something different, you will enter another world. But in order to be a rebel you have to know what you are rebelling against!

Facts About the Legs:

- The femur or thigh bone is the longest and strongest bone in the human skeleton.
- The femoral head is the distal (upper) end of the femur that inserts into the ball (acetabulum) of the hip joint.
- The greater trochanter is the protruding extremity of the upper femur that can be felt laterally at the hip. The primary function of the greater trochanter is to serve as an attachment site for several muscles in the hip region. Notably, it provides attachments for muscles responsible for abducting and rotating the thigh, including parts of the gluteus medius and gluteus minimus muscles, as well as the piriformis, obturator internus, and the superior and inferior gemelli. The greater trochanter also serves as an attachment point for hip ligaments, which contribute to the stability and integrity of the hip joint.
- The lesser trochanter is a bony projection from the shaft of the femur. It serves as the principal insertion site of the iliopsoas muscle.
- The hollow at the back of your knee (popliteus) is formed by a group of tendons that are attached on either side of the knee joint. These tendons extend from the hamstrings. The popliteus is an important contributor to overall knee stability and proper knee flexion.

Top Left: Anabella explains stretching the quadriceps muscles and the psoas, NYC, 2018
Bottom Left: Anabella explains stretching the hamstrings and dorsal muscles, Peridance Center NYC, 2018
Top Right: Anabella explains turnout, while feeling the trochanter, Peridance Center NYC, 2018
Bottom Right: Anabella explains turnout, while feeling the trochanter and the adductor muscles, Peridance Center NYC, 2018

Top: Anabella explaining feeling the trochanter while executing a *tendu a la second* in parallel, Peridance Center, NYC, 2018
Bottom Left: Anabella explains turnout and the relationship between the knee and the heel bone, Peridance Center, NYC, 2018.
Middle Right: Anabella explaining the pelvis alignment while feeling the trochanter in a turnout position on the floor, Peridance Center, NYC, 2018
Bottom Right: Outtake from dance film "Close to the Bone," Brooklyn, 2022

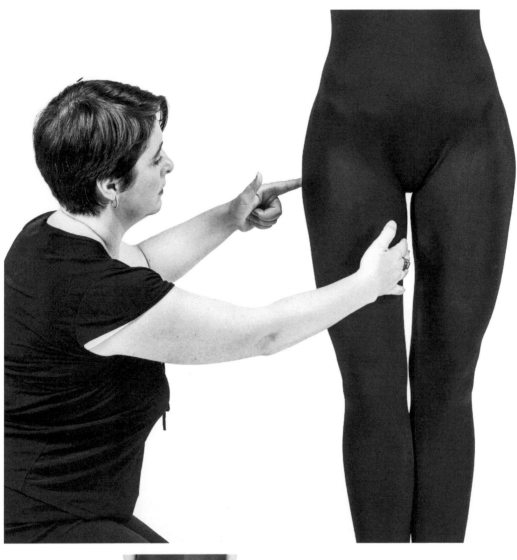

Top: Anabella explains the turnout, and the relationship between the deep six rotator muscles and the adductor muscles, 2015. Lauren Ohmer, dancer.

Bottom: Anabella explains turnout and the relationship between the trochanter and the heel bone, 2015. Lauren Ohmer, dancer.

Ankles & Feet

Here are some phrases that I use in class to guide students on the use of their feet:

- "The feet of a dancer are like the roots of a tree."
- "Strong feet provide the foundation for the whole body."
- "The feet are like the solid base of the Empire State Building. The basement must feel the weight of the body and connect us to what is underneath the building."
- "Your ankles provide stability for the entire architecture above them. They support the weight of the entire body."
- "Your feet and toes need to be more expressive than your hands."
- "Lick the floor with your feet!"
- To dance and perform efficiently, we need to know how to use the strength of our ankles, train our feet, be aware of our toes, and understand how weight is distributed on the soles of the feet.

Many dance styles and techniques require special shoes in their training. How can you be aware of your feet if they are hidden in a shoe? It is essential to have a separate practice and conditioning while barefoot!

If dance training is a healthy diet, you need some compensatory exercises to work specifically on your feet. Otherwise you are missing some essential vitamins!

Let's start by understanding a little anatomy.

Facts About the Feet

- The foot and ankle is a very complex mechanical structure comprising 26 bones, 34 joints, and over 100 muscles, tendons, and ligaments. All of these are interconnected with dependencies and limitations.
- The bones of the foot are: talus, calcaneus (heel bone), navicular, cuneiform, cuboid, metatarsals, and phalanges (see image on page 130).
- Weight is distributed differently when dancing flat versus demi-pointe (relevé).

Alignment & Placement

In the "perfect" relevé demi-pointe position, the center of the ankle should be aligned with the dancer's second toe, and the weight will be distributed between first and fifth toe. Focus on spreading the toes apart, and take care not to curl the toes in this position. While in demi-pointe, it is also important to work on the strength and stability of your ankles to reduce the risk of sprain, one of the most common injuries for a performer.

When we consider the foot flat on the floor, we need to visualize the three points that make contact with the ground. This "tripod of the foot" consists of the calcaneus or heel bone, fifth phalange, and first phalange.

When I'm explaining this idea, I find it helpful to emphasize the pressure that we need to execute on the floor. One must feel the pressure of the heel bone, the space between the fourth toe and the fifth toe, and the space between the first toe and the second toe. We must experience equal distribution of weight in this triangle between the heel and the toes.

Now let's consider the arch, which I think of as a cave. The curvature of the arch varies from person to person. The distribution of weight passes through the arch. Depending on the technique, you may be asked to support your weight in the middle of your foot, and some will ask you to keep your weight closer to the front of your foot, especially over your toes and metatarsals. This posture is important in readiness to attack or move fiercely in many techniques. For example, I worked with an opera director in Argentina who had all the actors hold their bodies in this posture, ready for action. You must be aware that this posture contracts the quadriceps and brings more tension in the hamstrings. No matter what you do, you must be able to adapt and change to meet the art form's needs.

My advice is to practice distributing weight evenly in the feet to establish a fundamental base, and when training in a specific technique, practice that technique's demands. For anatomical, strengthening, and stretching reasons, I encourage training with equal weight distribution because your muscles will be more relaxed. When practicing for performance, however, carry your weight toward the front. Performance and training are different states of being.

The Fascia & Understanding the Feet

Another element of the feet that deserves discussion is the fascia. In his book *Anatomy Trains*, Thomas Myers defines the "superficial back line" as a fascial plane that runs from our plantar fascia on the bottom of our feet all the way up the back and over the head to our eyebrows! "Superficial" simply refers to the fact that it's closer to the surface of your skin than other structures. This line is involved in our day-to-day actions and has a strong postural role in our bodies. (See illustration on page 131.)

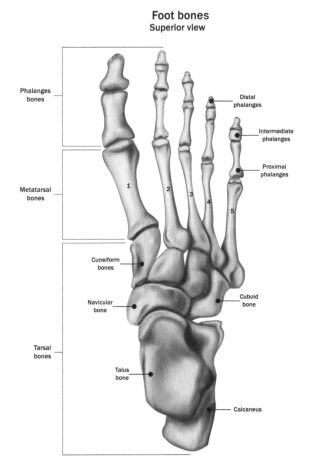

Foot bones
Superior view

To illustrate how this fascial line interacts, notice how it feels to bend over and touch your toes. Now take a tennis or golf ball (or a mobility ball), and roll the ball under the bottom of each foot for about 1 minute on each side. Now touch your toes again and notice the difference in feeling.

Understanding this should make you realize how important it is to be conscious of the "grounding" of your feet. Feet are one of the links in the chain that is the body. If you don't have a good understanding of the feet, you will not be able to maintain good alignment and communication with each body part.

The plantar fascia is a band of connective tissue that runs along the bottom surface of the foot. It acts as the main support for the medial longitudinal arch and therefore plays a key role in stabilizing the foot in actions that require pushing off from the ground for propulsion.

In daily life, the medial longitudinal is designed to allow the foot to compensate for an uneven surface and absorb shock. The lateral longitudinal helps with stability, and the anterior transverse aids in support and shock absorption, as well as stability and balance, especially in relevé.

I found this particularly well-summarized analysis of foot load during ballet dancers' gait in *Acta of Bioengineering and Biomechanics:* "In ballet dancers, weight distribution on the foot is notably different compared to non-dancers. Dancers show higher pressure on the medial edge of the forefoot and increased loading on the rearfoot, suggesting a unique distribution pattern likely caused by their specific training and movement techniques. This contrasts with non-dancers, who have a more even weight distribution across the foot during gait."

As humans, our natural distribution of weight is generally 60% hindfoot, 8% midfoot, 28% forefoot, and 4% on the toes, but as dancers, we must learn to shift our weight more forward and use the midfoot more as well. For example, in ballet training the idea is that the weight is very much over the forefoot so that relevé and jumps can be performed faster. The weight distribution of the body is then closer to the center line of balance for the pointe or demi-pointe position, when the dancer is working on a flat foot.

No matter which of the three leg positions you are using—parallel, turn-in, and turnout—awareness of the "superficial back line" should be the same. In turned out positions, some people might roll the feet inward or outward, but this is to be avoided because you can destabilize the body when you do this.

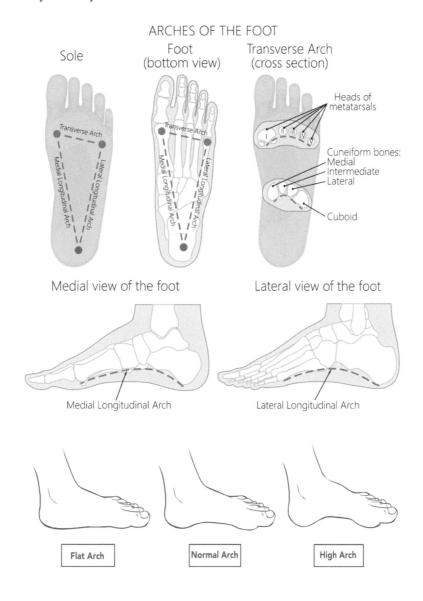

ARCHES OF THE FOOT

Sole · Foot (bottom view) · Transverse Arch (cross section)

Heads of metatarsals

Cuneiform bones: Medial, Intermediate, Lateral

Cuboid

Medial view of the foot · Lateral view of the foot

Medial Longitudinal Arch · Lateral Longitudinal Arch

Flat Arch · Normal Arch · High Arch

131

Supination, Pronation & Overpronation

Both terms involve your gait and how your weight is distributed as you walk or run. Supination means that when you walk, your weight tends to be more on the outside of your foot. Pronation means that when you walk, your weight tends to be more on the inside of your foot.

Overpronation happens when your gait eventually causes the arches of your feet to flatten more than they would normally. That puts strain on muscles, tendons, and ligaments that support your arches. Overpronation increases the risk of injury to the foot and leg.

Observing in detail how your feet are functioning will give you the key to understanding how to resolve your technical problems. Following are some exercises that can help you.

TRICEPS SURAE

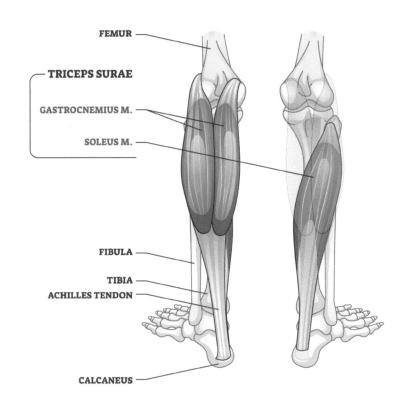

FEMUR

TRICEPS SURAE

GASTROCNEMIUS M.

SOLEUS M.

FIBULA

TIBIA

ACHILLES TENDON

CALCANEUS

PATHOLOGIES OF FOOT

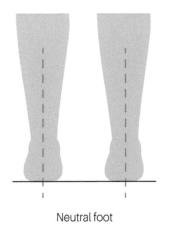

Neutral foot

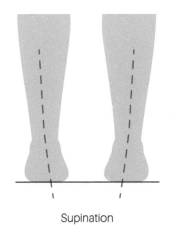

Supination

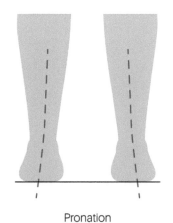

Pronation

Overpronation Exercises

If you overpronate, try these exercises while sitting in a chair:

- **Arch lifts:** With your foot on the ground, lift the arch without lifting your toes. Hold for three seconds, release, and repeat.
- **Foot rolls:** Place a tennis ball underneath where your big toe meets the foot. Lean forward to put weight on the ball while slowly rolling it toward your heel. Flex and point your toes to intensify the pressure.
- **Towel curls:** Place a towel under your foot. Without moving your heel, pull the towel toward you.
- **Marble pickups:** Place 10 to 15 marbles on the floor in front of you and use your toes to pick them up one at a time.
- **Big toe stretch:** Place your right ankle on your left knee. Grab your big toe and slowly pull it back. Hold for 15 seconds and release. Repeat on the other foot.

Supination Exercises

If you supinate, exercises designed to stretch the leg muscles can help by improving ankle range of motion.

- **Calf rolls:** Place a foam roller under your calf and roll back and forth for 30–60 seconds.
- **Ankle flexion:** Flex and release your ankles, or make small circles, for a few minutes per day.
- **Foot pulls:** Place a resistance band around the ball of your foot and pull back lightly.
- **Calf raises:** While standing, do 10 to 15 calf raises. You can also do these on a stair or step.

Flat Feet

Flat feet is a common condition, also known as flatfoot, in which the arches on the inside of the feet flatten when pressure is put on them. When people with flat feet stand up, the feet point outward, and the entire soles of the feet fall and touch the floor. Flat feet can occur when the arches don't develop during childhood. It can also develop later in life after an injury or from the simple wear-and-tear stresses of age.

Exercises for Flat Feet

- **Golf ball roll:** Sit on a chair with your feet firmly on the ground. Place a golf ball under the foot, and roll it forward and back under the arch of the foot for 2 minutes to stretch the plantar fascia ligament.

Tight Achilles Tendon

A tight Achilles tendon will encourage the foot to roll inward. The heel cord stretch will stretch the Achilles tendon and posterior calf muscles. To perform heel cord stretching, a person should:

- Stand facing a wall and place one hand on the wall at eye level.
- Place the leg that needs stretching approximately one step behind the other leg, and plant the heel firmly on the ground.
- Bend the knee of the front leg until you feel a stretch in the back leg.
- Hold for 30 seconds and then rest for 30 seconds.
- Repeat nine times. It is essential to avoid arching the back and to keep it straight.

Foot Health

If you suffer from flat feet, ongoing foot or ankle pain, numbness, tingling, loss of function, or an injury, you should see a podiatrist. This medical professional can fully diagnose your foot health problems and prescribe custom orthotics, medication, and other therapies to correct your feet.

General Foot & Ankle Exercises

- **Ankle Circles.** Sit or lie down comfortably and lift one or both feet off the ground. Gently rotate your ankle in a circular motion, clockwise and counterclockwise, thinking that you are tracing the circle with the big toe. This exercise improves ankle mobility and enhances blood circulation.
- **Calf Raises.** Strong calf muscles play a significant role in stabilizing the ankle joint. Stand with your feet hip-width apart and slowly raise your heels off the ground, lifting your body weight onto your toes. Lower your heels back down and repeat. Gradually increase the number of repetitions to build calf strength and ankle stability.
- **Resistance Band or TheraBand Exercises.** Incorporating resistance bands into your workout routine can enhance ankle strength and heal a swollen ankle injury. Wrap a resistance band around your forefoot. Flex your foot against the band's resistance, then point it away from you.
- **Towel Scrunches.** Place a small towel on the floor and stand on it with your toes. Use your toes to scrunch the towel toward you, then release it. This exercise strengthens the muscles in your toes, which are essential for balance and ankle stability.
- **Single-Leg Balancing.** Balancing on one leg can help improve ankle stability and proprioception. To heal an ankle injured from running, stand on one foot and hold the position for as long as possible without losing balance. As you progress, close your eyes or introduce unstable surfaces, like a foam pad, to make the exercise more challenging.

Top: Anabella explains how to point the feet while keeping proper alignment of the ankles, 2015. Lauren Ohmer, dancer.

Middle: Anabella explains how to feel the fascia underneath the sole of the foot, 2015. Lauren Ohmer, dancer.

Bottom: Anabella explains how to spread and lengthen the toes, 2015. Lauren Ohmer, dancer.

- **Alphabet Exercises.** Sit down and lift one leg off the ground. Imagine you are drawing the letters of the alphabet with your big toe. This exercise engages various ankle muscles and promotes flexibility.
- **Ankle Dorsiflexion Stretch.** Sit on the floor with your legs extended. Loop a resistance band around the ball of one foot and gently pull the band toward you. Hold the stretch for 15-30 seconds and repeat on the other side. This exercise helps maintain flexibility in the ankle joint.
- **Achilles Tendon Stretch.** Stand facing a wall and place your hands on it for support. Take a step back with one leg, keeping it straight. Bend the front knee and lean forward slightly to feel a stretch in the calf and Achilles tendon. Hold for 15-30 seconds on each leg.

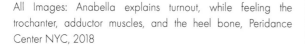

All Images: Anabella explains turnout, while feeling the trochanter, adductor muscles, and the heel bone, Peridance Center NYC, 2018

Mind as Muscle

We think a lot about physical movements, such as how high we can jump, how many turns we can do, how flexible we are, or how strong we are. But what happens with the mind? **The mind is also a muscle we must train.**

The practice of memorization in dance training is one I think we, as teachers, need to critically evaluate. In reality, memorization is not just the practice of memorizing as fast as possible but, rather, picking up phrases of movement and associating those phrases with imagination and expression. We must empower the dancer to use the mind as a tool and to be creative with it.

Many dancers who have worked with me over the years said that they become smarter working with the methodology I use, so I want to share it with you here.

Sometimes I make the performers rehearse the same movement over and over again, changing the variables: Example: repeat it 3 times but backwards, going from the end to the beginning of the movement phrase. Also helpful is to have a dancer transfer the movement from one part of the body to another (i.e., feet to hands) or change the dynamics and texture of the movements. I treat the class material like an experimentation lab, where dancers and performers can play with movement material and manipulate principles of movements.

Improvisation is an important tool to train the imagination, creativity, and the mind! Every time that I assign improvisation in class or rehearsal, I always tell the dancers that every time they improvise, they need to remember what they did. Why? To train their memory! They need to be able to reproduce at least eighty percent of what they improvised exactly the same way as when they first did it. It's hard, and it's essential to practice! Sometimes when you improvise you get "possessed," and you dance unconsciously. However, I challenge my dancers to be fully aware of their senses. It is a part of dance training, this ability to memorize. **That is why we write books or make videos about dance—to try to capture the dance or at least trace the impulses that generated that dance. But the reality is that the mind and senses of a dancer keep the dance alive.**

Yes, we take notes in rehearsal, there is a lot of notation. But it is the dancer who really needs to train mentally in order to memorize thousands of choreographies and phrases of movement. I think it is important to address that factor.

I'm interested in creating dances and training performers who value their creations. They must be able to build upon other dances they've created or seen, and do research about them, relying on their memory. I don't want to create "disposable" and "forgetable" dancers or dances.

Many dancers are a little lazy, unfortunately, so they rely on notes and they rely on videos. As a choreographer, sometimes even I do not perfectly remember the counts or accents that we built, but I remember the space, and I have to remember (or it's important to remember) eighty percent of the material.

Another component of the mind that we must cultivate is our ability to react quickly. As a dancer, you are often trained to be able to react very quickly physically but not necessarily mentally. I remember I was a bit like Sleeping Beauty when it came to reacting spontaneously in an intellectual way. Reacting doesn't just imply physically. It is also a form of intellectual response.

Left: Self-portrait, Anabella Lenzu, 2020
Right: Self-portrait, Anabella Lenzu, 2020

Don't forget: **Dance is also an intellectual field!** The mind is a very important tool in the world of dance. If you are a dancer or a choreographer, you must have a strong mind and a good memory, and you must be able to make associations and react quickly.

What can we do to encourage this type of mental growth? In teaching, I emphasize critical thinking and personal life experience as it relates to dance. In all my classes, whether they are theoretical or practical, I make performers read and research more than they thought possible.

Simple exercises to train the mind as a muscle may include:

1. Ask your students to do a few basic movements or phrases to the right, then immediately to the left without first marking through it. Then ask them to try it en dehors and en dedans and/or from the beginning to the end and vice versa.
2. Ask your students to do phrases A, B, and C. Then ask them to do the phrases in a different order, for example C, B, A, or B, A, C, with only one minute to think about it in advance.

Top: "The Night That You Stopped Acting/ La Noche que dejaste de Actuar" performance at Center for Performance Research, 2019
Bottom Images: "No More Beautiful Dances" performance at La Mama Moves Festival, NYC, 2018

Form & Intention

It is my impression that many dancers are worried about the idea of form, or how things look from the outside. **Form is a result of a direction, an intention, and an organization of energy. Energy creates the form of a movement. Intention liberates the energy that creates the form of a movement.**

If I ask someone to stand in parallel position with their feet and arms in ballet's fifth position, they will immediately produce the shape, or form, but what happens if I make them first understand how the energy travels circularly from the T4 to their fingers to create the arms in the fifth position of ballet? I see a remarkable difference. Form is bound to intention. I like to think that good dancers understand this relationship. That's why I teach principles and intentions and meaningful gestures!

An example of form would be asking a dancer to place their arm at a 90-degree line or angle in relation to their spine. Many times, when I work with students on their arms, they cannot tell if their arm is at a 90-degree angle in relation to their spine. Sometimes to achieve that form you need to use the mirror. It takes most students years to understand what it feels like to have the arm at a 90-degree angle to the spine with their eyes open, with eyes closed, on the floor, and standing up.

Ultimately, the accurate expression comes from an internal awareness of how energy flows in your body and how you produce lines and shapes. To train this sensibility, we sometimes need the mirror to affirm that we actually look the way we feel we look. As a teacher you need to constantly remind your student of where their body is in the kinesphere, as well as in relation to the physical space they are in. The student must eventually understand that the internal organization of their energy creates the form.

It is important to understand the shapes you produce with your body. The way you "architect" your body has an effect on you and on your audience. With each shape, you create a symbol for both you and the audience to read. This idea returns to the principle that Motion Creates Emotion, and Emotion Creates Motion. This principle goes hand in hand with François Delsarte's concept that, "Every gesture is expressive of something. ...It is preceded by and given birth by a thought, a feeling, an emotion, a purpose, a design or a motive."

When you perform with your arms curved in ballet's fifth position, you and your audience do not feel the same as when you perform with your arms in a parallel line perpendicular to the ceiling. What is the difference between a curve and a line? This difference evokes something internally and externally.

Related to form is an awareness and familiarity with symmetry and asymmetry. It is important that you understand these concepts to have full access to your ability to create shapes. No human is perfectly symmetrical. One leg might be shorter than the other, one hip higher than the other; scoliosis, or rotation in our torso, is among the infinite different physical idiosyncrasies. Nonetheless, we need to learn how to work as symmetrically as possible to develop supportive muscles that allow energy to flow freely and prevent injuries. Practically, this means that when we are doing any type of exercise, we must try to do it as symmetrically as possible. If we know that we are weaker or more flexible on one side, for example, we will work to cultivate symmetry of both sides by doing additional exercises.

A simple exercise to practice symmetry is to choose a new starting point. Instead of always starting an exercise with the right side (a tendency in many dance classes), start with the left. This simple adjustment can have a significant impact on your technique. The first time we do an exercise, it is largely to understand the mechanisms by which the physical movements requested can be performed. The second time and each time thereafter allows us to work more and more deeply on different physical, mental, and spiritual concepts. As a consequence, if we always start with the right side, we get to practice working deeply only on the left, cultivating asymmetry. As such, just alternating which side we start with can go a long way toward achieving symmetry.

Some techniques focus more on a sense of symmetry, whereas others focus more on a sense of asymmetry. Some techniques emphasize releasing shapes, and some are more focused on creating shapes. In ballet class, you are practicing symmetrical positions all the time because that particular technique is interested in expression of lines. However, you may also be learning a modern dance technique, where shapes are more asymmetrical. Both appear different, and you must understand the motivation for each technique's gestures in order to be able to produce it. Thus, the training of a dancer must cultivate the ability to access both symmetry and asymmetry to adapt to different techniques or styles.

We dancers often think we must conform to a particular aesthetic or form
to be successful, but in reality there are many ways to be a dance or performance artist.
You may be passionate about an existing aesthetic or form and excel in it.

Also, it is important to remember that the beginning of any dance technique, style, or new dance practice actually came about because a new generation broke from an existing form and made a new one. For example, modern dance was a rebellion against ballet aesthetics, and postmodern dance was a rebellion against modernism. All these styles started by challenging ideas of what was beautiful or functional or representative at a different moment in time and space. Ideas about what looks good and what shapes are acceptable evolve naturally and inevitably over time.

As new techniques progress, patterns develop and a basic vernacular of particular shapes and forms starts to build. Then the cycle begins again! For example, pioneers of modern dance, after rebelling against ballet technique ended up creating new techniques with distinctive shapes and forms, which later became even more formalized than ballet, which in turn led to the birth of postmodern dance.

An example of this is the German impressionistic dancer and choreographer Mary Wigman. When we read any of Mary Wigman's works, we find that her notions of beauty were very different from those of her American dance predecessors. Her process started from an internal motivation to challenge existing ideas about shape and form. Her "forms" come from internal motivation.

Let's look at another common situation in which a teacher or choreographer directs you to perform shapes without giving you information about their motivation. In that case, the dancer creates their own motivation and intention. When I work with trusted dancers in my company, especially when I teach repertory, I sometimes teach just shapes and the technique of the movement, but I give the dancers no information about the intention behind the movement. I do this so I do not impinge on the dancers' freedom to create their own stories. Sometimes I do the opposite. I start by giving the dancers information about the motivation for the movement, such as, "I need a movement that reflects that my dancer is melting." I ask my dancer to imagine that they are clay or wax and are close to a fire, so they are melting. In this instance, the ultimate melting shape comes from motivation.

A few years ago I was teaching a section of my repertory choreography *Pachamama: Mother World*, which is based on a ritual of initiation from an indigenous tribe in Ushuaia, Argentina. This ritual has many different characters or masks that the actors/dancers performed with during the rituals. One character is similar to a stereotypical macho man, very strong and threatening to women and children. I was teaching the repertory through the movement, and I made each person create their own "masculine energy character" that would terrify the audience. One woman chose to create a "feminine energy character" instead, so her performance was totally different from the others. She chose her own story and her own motivation. One of my assistants said, "But, Anabella! It is completely wrong!" I said, "No, it is fine because she is still doing the correct choreography. She has simply chosen a different energy and story because I gave her the freedom to do so." The dancer frightened the audience, and that was exactly what I wanted! It was a very clear example of how a choreographer can use freedom to design intention and motivation behind gestures.

A dancer who tends to be more creative usually has had more training in creating their own motivation and intention behind movements. A dancer who has learned to copy shapes is usually more adept at quickly memorizing shapes and filling in the gaps. **I feel it is very important for dancers to take repertory workshops to understand different choreographers' ways of thinking and structuring ideas and practices.**

It's as if you're an actor and you're asked to learn Shakespeare's *Hamlet*. You create your own interpretation of the character from your own external and internal research. The director shapes you and guides you in this creative search. The same thing can happen when you learn an existing piece of choreography or repertory piece. The choreographer guides you in your interpretation of the work. It's very different from working on a piece that the choreographer is newly developing. In that case, the dancers are the choreographer's artistic material—as paint is to the painter—so the dancer's motivation influences new choreographic shapes. It's important to have both skills. That is why I recommend improvisation as an important tool through which students can learn how to create their own forms on a regular basis.

Breath

It wasn't until I was 18 years old and was working as a choreographer with an opera director, using the François Delsarte technique that I started to understand breath in dancing. Looking back, it was a little too late in my development to have discovered this, but such is life. Until that point, as strange as it sounds, I had always felt that it was "unnatural" to breathe because in ballet you try not to make any breathing noise, and many times I found myself holding my breath at the hardest technical moments.

When I heard modern dancers breathing, I thought, "Why are they making so much noise? Do they really need it? Are they exaggerating, or is it a psychological release?"

We started to work on the Delsarte methods while I was a guest choreographer for the restaging of Leoncavallo's opera *Pagliacci* in Casa della Opera in Buenos Aires. The opera director and I talked a lot about breath, which opened my mind and gave me some answers— as well as new questions!

We worked a lot on the breath of the dancers and the singers. It was fascinating for me to be able to "score" the dancers' breath for the entire production. We had rehearsals just for breath, which changed things completely for me. Now, when I see a dancer who is not breathing properly, I feel that the dancer is like a puppet on stage, lifeless. If you don't breathe, you cannot move properly. The breath is the fuel for your muscles and for your brain as well. I recommend reading the chapter on Teaching Breath, Voice, and Muscular Drama (see Chapter 7, page 62) to complement this chapter.

The breath of the dancer is different from the breath of a singer, actor, or musician. In my experience as a teacher, when you breathe, you serve the movement and the material that you are performing. There are no rules about how to breathe—just conscientious choices of how and why to breathe. Taking in oxygen slowly or quickly changes the dynamics of your movements, how energy emanates from your body, your muscular effort, and, well, just about everything!

I trained for years in hatha yoga, where the goal was to breathe "healthy," using only the nostrils. In dance, however, the goal is to achieve expression, communication, entertainment, and art-making itself! So breath training, in our case, is like having many colors to choose from when painting. If I breathe only through my nostrils, as in yoga, I do not have access to oxygen quickly enough to fuel my movements. When you dance, you need to have enough oxygen to react and attack.

You are like a Ferrari. As soon as you put your foot on the gas, you need to go.

If you're breathing only through your tiny nostrils, it takes longer for oxygen to reach your muscles than it does if you breathe through your mouth. This doesn't mean you must open your mouth like a fish to inhale and exhale, but oxygen needs to move in and out of your body freely and quickly.

When we do exercises in my classes or workshops, we work on how different breathing techniques affect the performance of a phrase of movement. For example, we might try breathing just through the nose or just through the mouth. Maybe we try breathing as little as possible or as much as possible. Each version is dramatically different. Breathing clarifies, distracts from, or even explicitly changes the choreographic intent.

In 1999, I attended a performance by the Martha Graham Company performing *Act of Life* at the Joyce Theater in New York City. All the dancers wore yellow unitards and began the piece by sitting on the floor. Then they started to

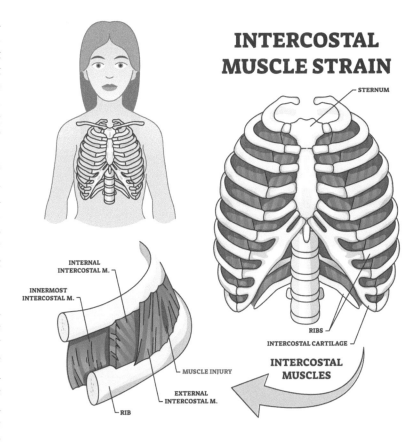

THE DIAPHRAGM FUNCTIONS
IN BREATHING

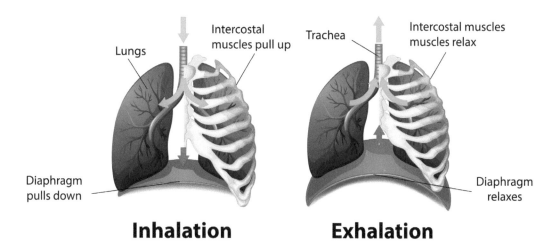

Lungs

Intercostal muscles pull up

Trachea

Intercostal muscles muscles relax

Diaphragm pulls down

Diaphragm relaxes

Inhalation   **Exhalation**

MECHANISM OF
BREATHING

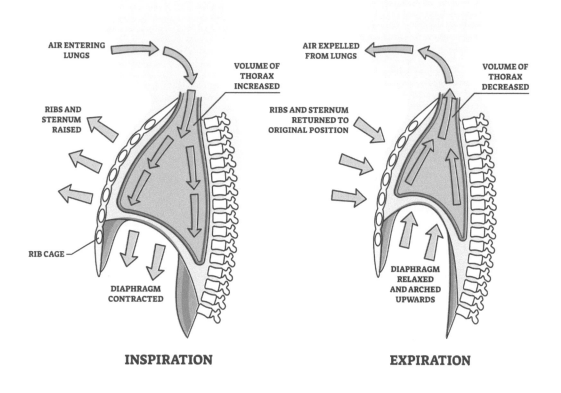

AIR ENTERING LUNGS

VOLUME OF THORAX INCREASED

RIBS AND STERNUM RAISED

AIR EXPELLED FROM LUNGS

VOLUME OF THORAX DECREASED

RIBS AND STERNUM RETURNED TO ORIGINAL POSITION

RIB CAGE

DIAPHRAGM CONTRACTED

DIAPHRAGM RELAXED AND ARCHED UPWARDS

INSPIRATION   **EXPIRATION**

"Pachamama: Mother World" performance at Sheen Center, NYC, 2016

do all the Graham floor work/techniques, spirals, bounces, etc. There was a moment when I realized that everyone in the entire theater—all the dancers on stage and everyone in the audience—was breathing together in sync, at the same rhythm. We shared the same air. We shared the environment. Communication between the dancers and the audience was through the breath. It was shared, synchronized breathing, and it was magical.

When you're in the audience for a performance by the Pina Bausch Company—even if you sit at the very rear of the theater—you see and hear the dancers breathing because breath is a synonym for life, effort, and ecstasy!

One exercise to help understand breath is to place the palms of your hands on your back and try to get your fingers to cover as much surface of your ribs and lungs as you can. Then breathe into the space covered by your hands, expand your rib cage to the sides and back. You should feel the articulation of the rib cage on the vertebrae, as well as the movement between the vertebrae themselves. You can do this exercise with a partner as well.

An exercise that uses the intercostal muscles between the ribs helps students understand that there are different kinds of breath. You can breathe with the top, the middle part, or the bottom part of your lungs. How you breath depends on what the choreographer requires and how slow or fast the movements need to be. Regardless of which part of the lungs you use, your ribs should always be expanding sideways when you breathe. I never see a dancer breathing with their belly unless it is choreographed because you generally don't have time for such a deep breath. However, when dancers breathe only with the top of their lungs, when it comes time for curtain calls, they are often so out of breath that I feel they need oxygen masks!

We need to practice using the middle section of the lungs, as well as expanding the rib cage sideways and to the back. Again, unless a choreographer asks you to do a lot of movement with the chest, you are probably breathing into just the top of your lungs and you may be in danger of hyperventilating. It is a lot to ask of the heart too. If you breathe with your belly, you are most likely disrupting the choreographic aesthetic unless the choreographer/director wants to see the movement of your abdominals. On stage, most of the breath happens in the middle part of your lungs.

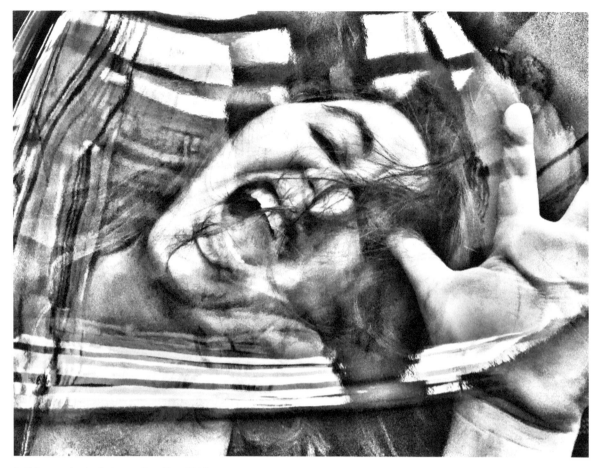

Self-Portrait, Anabella Lenzu, Brooklyn, 2020

It makes you think more lyrically when you imagine that your lungs are like balloons that support and sustain you. It becomes easier to balance, particularly when you work in techniques that switch frequently between being off balance and on balance.

Depending on the choreography, you may or may not hear dancers or performers breathing on stage. It is up to the choreographer or director and their own aesthetic. Sometimes it is important to hear the breath and sometimes it is not. In Pina Bausch's production of *The Rite of Spring*, when the whole group is dancing, one woman in the front is frightened and lets out an exaggerated breath that looks and feels utterly natural. It is stunning and perfectly communicates life and death.

Always be aware that the breath is also "score." But whether it is audible or not, you definitely must have a heightened consciousness of your breath. You don't breathe the same way when you do a grand plié that you do when you kick your leg. You inhale and exhale at different times and in different amounts. It has an impact on you as an interpreter of movements. It gives you different sensations, different weight, and different impulses.

We know that when we exhale and release air, the effect on the body is to be more grounded. So if you want to fall to the ground sideways and you really want to access that fall, you will exhale with the movement. But if you want to fall and recover very lightly, you inhale at the same time as you fall. You can see that breath can be parallel or opposite to your movement,

145

depending on what you want to achieve. Training your breath must be part of the technique that you learn in every dance class!

In some ways, the dance teacher is like a photographer reacting to the environment, seeing, capturing, and responding to what is happening. Even students in early childhood should begin training their breath along with rhythm. It is easier to move when you are aware of your breath. Dancers tend to accumulate tension and shorten their breath. When I see a dancer unable to complete a turn, for example, the correction that often makes the difference is working with their breathing. If you find that you can't jump high enough at a certain point in a dance, it might be because you are inhaling when you should be exhaling, etc.

Explore the breath in dance class! It is really fun to do for both teacher and students because there is no universal answer. It all depends on what you want to achieve. It is impossible to work on everything or teach everything in one class or one workshop. As a dancer, if you want to work on something, it is going to take time. Now that you know that these different elements exist, ignore them at your peril!

Here are some facts about the respiratory muscles:

- The primary respiratory muscles are the diaphragm and external intercostals.
- The accessory muscles used to inhale are: the sternocleidomastoid; the scalenus anterior, medius, and posterior; the pectoralis major and minor; the inferior fibers of serratus anterior, and latissimus dorsi. The serratus posterior superior and the iliocostalis cervicis may also help in breathing.
- The accessory muscles used to exhale are: the abdominal muscles: rectus abdominis, external oblique, internal oblique, and transversus abdominis.
- The iliocostalis and longissimus fibers, the serratus posterior inferior, and quadratus lumborum are the accessory muscles that are recruited during exercise because of increased metabolic need. They are also used when the respiratory system is in dysfunction.

Eye & Focus

Different techniques use the face, especially the eyes, to a greater or lesser degree. I'm sure everyone is familiar with the phrase "The eyes are the windows to the soul." We use our eyes as a medium of expression and communication.

As dancers or performers, when we train or practice, we rarely think about visual focus. **For me, the eyes have a direct energy connection to the spine unless you have to focus your work inwardly following the guidance of the choreographer or director.** That is why I find it so interesting to compare disciplines, so we can see how narrowly we sometimes use our tools as dancers or performers.

When I began my work with opera and theater directors, I started to think about breath, the use of the eyes, and visual focus. This was a big turning point for me. It is not like the ballet in which there are different schools of technique—Russian, French, etc.—with different positions as well as different focus, or eye movements, that accompany the arm movements.

We can apply the three circles of energy methodology to eyes and focus. I suggest referring to Chapter 8, pages 180-183.

"Sangre y Arena" performance at DMAC, NYC, 2012. Julia Lindpaintner, dancer

How do our eyes absorb the environment and react to it? How are our eyes part of our non-verbal communication? Regardless of what technique class I am teaching, I often instruct dancers to close their eyes to understand that the eyes exist and serve a purpose. Sometimes it is almost like we forget that we have a body, and we think the head and eyes are unimportant. When we close our eyes, we can understand that our eyes are not the center of our energy. Alignment happens regardless of whether the eyes are open or closed. Sometimes people lose their proprioception when their eyes are closed. They do not know where they are, they cannot hold their balance, they do not understand alignment, and they do not understand gravity. Some people have the opposite response. When they close their eyes they feel self-confident, and they feel very present in their bodies, so when they open their eyes, it feels like everything disappears.

I advise dancers that when you are training, close your eyes once in a while, even if the teacher says not to do so and even when you are jumping and turning and running, though you must not collapse on the floor or collide with another dancer! Moving with closed eyes will give you another type of knowledge. It lets you experience being in yourself and outside of yourself. It is best to start slowly with this experiment, perhaps at the barre or on the floor with phrases of movement that don't travel in space.

I like to use the following example to help students understand this idea. It is a funny one, but everybody relates to it. Imagine you are kissing your new boyfriend or girlfriend, and your old boyfriend or girlfriend is looking at you. You are in a very close and intimate relationship with your new partner, but then out of the corner of your eye you are aware that your ex is

Top: Anabella teaching focus, Peridance Center, NYC, 2017
Bottom: Self-Portraits, Anabella Lenzu, 2020

watching you, so you "perform" for them. That is what happens when you are in an intimate relationship with yourself while an audience is watching you. Your awareness of two viewpoints must be engaged all the time. Practice with your eyes open and closed. Think of these two viewpoints being active at the same time. One hopes they are parallel to each other and not perpendicular. Perpendicular would be the creative process being split in two as you express one idea with two different actions for two different viewers—the audience and yourself. This won't work, in my opinion!

If you are aware of and know how to use your visual tools, you can explore. How will you apply this knowledge of fundamental awareness? It does not matter if you are a beginner, intermediate, or professional dancer. If you have this knowledge, what are you going to do about it? I find it fascinating to study the different cultures that developed a serious practice of facial and eye expression in performance arts, like the Asian theatrical cultures of the Peking Opera, Indian Odissi and Kathakali dance, Balinese dance, Japanese Buyo dance, Kabuki, Butoh, etc.

CHAPTER 9.
ADVICE FOR STUDENTS

Self-Reflection and Responsibility

At the end of the day, I think a student's success reflects their thirst and hunger to learn. A student will learn no matter what, regardless of whether you have a good or bad teacher, if you are in a small town, or live in one of the world's capitals. You will learn anyway. Your success as a student is not about institutions. Let me state this as clearly as I can: I do not believe that a university, an academy, or a dance studio can create artists. I do not believe it. I think that artistry arises from within the person. Each of us has our own path. I have had a lot of education, but more than half of my education came from me, alone, in a dance studio, inspired by books, articles, and videos. I've certainly been inspired by others and by the encouragement of dear mentors, but a big part of my journey has been being all by myself.

There is no right way to become a dance artist. I've often heard people say, "Oh, I feel like I never completed my technical training because I never studied at a university!" or "I started dancing too late!" I feel we make a lot of excuses for ourselves, and we believe in limitations about ourselves that just aren't true.

From 17 to 22 years old, I trained in daily ballet technique alone in my studio in Bahia Blanca, Argentina, accompanied by my assistant, Soledad. I would take classes and record myself and watch these videos later. I became aware of what I could and couldn't do. I trained this way so I could see myself as objectively as possible, to bridge the gap between how I felt doing a certain movement and what the camera captured. I said to myself, "Okay, Anabella, you are not going to be a prima ballerina. You are not going to be in the American Ballet Theatre or the Royal Ballet." I saw it plainly, but I did not accept it as a failure. First, I recognized that I did not have the spirit to work in the way that ballet requires. I needed to speak about my own history and my own culture. I was not a good fit for dancing the ballet fairy tales. I studied and performed ballet repertory but only as a way to study dance composition and to understand the logic behind a solo or an ensemble piece. I also persevered in challenging myself technically as a dancer to attempt virtuosic execution, and I recognized that I wasn't meant to go down that path.

I learned something very valuable from all this hard work: I found that I was more interested in teaching and choreographing than I was in dancing ballet or for an existing dance company. For me, ballet was like studying the Latin language, and I learned the structures, the principles, the rules of this classical dance language.

At the beginning, I was afraid of taking a different path, but I thought, "I will start to make my own choreography. I am going to start talking about the things that are important and interesting to me that I could not find in the work of other choreographers." I started to develop my own language as a choreographer, my own dance practices.

There is a lot of fear involved with making choices, and we often use this fear as an excuse. I could have said, "I am not going to be a dancer," but instead I said, "I like dance and there is not just one way of doing things. I will do what works for me."

When I realized I would not dance for a big ballet company like Teatro Colón, I decided not to let it affect me. There are amazing dancers in Teatro Colón, and for a time I thought if I was

"Listen to Your Mother" performance at La Mama Moves Festival, NYC, 2024

not one of them I wasn't fulfilling my dreams, but then I understood it was not for me, and that was fine. In many ways, I was able to feel a strong sense of security in my choice because of my family and my education. My high school experience (at Escuela Normal Superior, an extension of the Universidad del Sur in Bahia Blanca, where I obtained my Bachelor in Pedagogy and Humanities) taught me how to be critical and realistic. It taught me to use self-reflection to see myself for who I am and to bear responsibility for my own choices.

On this road, I learned how to see myself from the outside as an artist. This is very important. As a person, how do you appear from the outside, to others? Sometimes we make decision-making more complex than it really is. I think it comes down to fear. We are living in fear: fear of failure, fear of being confused, fear to exist. It's our culture. Sometimes we make decisions out of fear, not because it's actually what we want to do. The same thing is true of relationships or work. However, we must recognize when we need to take time for a period of reflection before we make a decision and take action. That reflection can give us strength and security so we need not be full of fear. **This is what my career and life experience have taught me: to be fearless to transform and evolve.**

Learning Self-Discipline

Your teachers are not responsible for your education. You are responsible. I had good teachers, but I did not learn anything from some of them. Likewise, I had bad teachers from whom I learned a great deal. It is important that you know what your body, mind, and spirit or heart need.

At some point, I realized I needed to train myself, and I needed to create. So, for three years I worked for five and six hours a day by myself and with my assistant in my Bahia Blanca studio, L'Atelier Centro Creativo de Danza. I also taught open classes to children and adults. I learned by experimenting. I knew I wouldn't understand all of the theories my earlier teachers talked about until I first practiced them myself, and I later shared my discoveries with others.

Once a week during those years of self-training, I recorded my solo classes. I would wait one week, and then I would sit down with my assistant and view the video of myself. I took notes about the mechanics of my body, listing the things that I wanted to improve. I incorporated those notes into lessons in my personal training, which consisted of barre training of different durations (sometimes 20 minutes, sometimes two hours), depending on what technical aspects I sought to improve, then center work, then point work, and then repertory. After a short break or quick lunch, I rehearsed my own choreography.

My learning environment was very particular because I was working only with my assistant, who was in the early stages of learning ballet technique. I created sequences and exercises that allowed us both to explore new footwork or experiment with arm positions not normally used in traditional port de bras (such as making reverse or diagonal circles). I used pop and rock music instead of classical. I applied the ballet vocabulary and principles, but I changed the pace and mood to challenge us creatively, emotionally, and muscularly!

Top: "The Night That You Stopped Acting/ La Noche que dejaste de actuar" performance at Center for Performance Research, Brooklyn, 2019
Right: Anabella teaching "My Body, My Country" body mapping workshop at Columbia University, NYC, 2019

A lot of the time as a dancer, you are taking so many classes and trying to fulfill other people's ideas that you do not have time for yourself to experiment. You need guidance

Both Images: "Listen to Your Mother" performance at La Mama Moves Festival, NYC, 2024

from mentors and teachers to know that you are on the right path, but then you also need time for yourself. Every artist does. One problem is that sometimes we dancers are afraid to work alone, and we depend too much on group training. We do need teachers to give us their perspectives, but artists need to go a step further to apply these perspectives directly to themselves.

I had wonderful mentors and teachers, of course, and I am eternally thankful to them for their gifts, but things "clicked" when I worked by myself in my studio because I was listening carefully only to myself. I think that ability to be by yourself in the studio comes with professionalism. As a 17-year-old I was a very mature dancer artistically and technically, so it made sense for me. Each person follows a different path, but I recommend that dancers take time to be alone in the studio to work on themselves physically, take chances creatively, and push themselves intellectually.

At least once or twice a week, take some time to learn who you are. Then you can come back to your mentors and teachers with questions and concerns. But you must spend time on your own!

See Teaching Self-Discipline in Chapter 7, starting on page 49 for more on this topic!

When to Start Training

The best age to start dance training is? As soon as possible! Whether you have a child who loves to move, or you are a teenager, or adult, your body, mind, and heart will tell you when to start. Weekly dance training is the best way for a person to acquire self-knowledge and to learn about discipline, commitment, self-respect and more.

Dance helps you to become aware of your passions and strengths, and it awakens creative impulses. Dance training helps to connect or reconnect people with joy and fullness.

I advise everyone to dance, to find your own style or technique. Try every dance language until your heart is fulfilled.

I first enrolled my kids in dance class when they were 18 months old. They didn't necessarily learn how to dance, but they moved around and played with props and were moved by the music. They learned how to harmoniously live in community dancing with their classmates. They had fun!

Dance, for me, is a union of a person with her interior. It is a communion with yourself, with others, with the environment, and with life. One can understand life through dance. I believe the dance class is a time to enjoy, work, think, and increase one's self-confidence.

Training

Training is a creative process. It is also a process of selection. You must be selective about your training choices. You must evaluate the pros and cons of being a "butterfly" student, going from school to school, from teacher to teacher, from technique to technique. Will you join a two-year professional program where you will have the same teachers for the duration of the program, or will you take a four-year program in a college or university department?

I hope you believe me when I tell you that the shorter way is not always the right answer for a dancer or choreographer's career. On a solid foundation, you can build a solid profession. You will have deep knowledge, not superficial information.

What can help you is thinking about your goals. How do you see yourself in five or 10 years? What are the steps to follow?

When you train, you create a map of your body, a map of your choices. You create yourself as a performer in so many ways. Besides training your body, you must train your critical thinking. You must discern between deep and shallow training.

In training, you must first learn what your tools are.

Training strengthens your best qualities and can magnify your weaknesses! As I was preparing to write this chapter, I was reminiscing about my training and performance experiences.

- When I began, I took at least one class per day, five days per week, in ballet and Spanish folk dances or flamenco, plus I performed four to 10 times a year, sometimes more.
- In my teens, I took either two classes or one three- to four-hour class every day, six days a week, to complement my performance work, and I performed at least 12 times a year.
- In my 20s, it was two classes a day five days per week, plus long rehearsals and improvisational experiments. I performed two or three times per week, depending on tours, seasons, and international festivals. Apart from dancing, I also started writing, and during 1998–2001, I was the editor in chief of *Nexos de la Cultura Bahiense Magazine* in Argentina.
- In my 30s, I became a mother of two children, and I fully dedicated myself to my choreography. I trained on my own three times a week, occasionally taking workshops with renowned teachers and choreographers, and I performed two or three times a month. I spent most of my time investigating, deepening my choreographic practices through improvisation with my company members. I continued to write articles, interviews, and reviews for art and dance magazines. I published my first book, *Unveiling Motion and Emotion*.
- Now that I'm in my 40s, I continue my choreographic journey and write for art and dance magazines. I keep training on my own, at home at my own pace, with all the resources and information I have gathered over these 35 years of teaching.

Now, looking at the advancing dawn of my 50s, I write this book for you and keep my choreographic practices sharp for the stage and for screendance.

Depending on your personal specifics, such as your age and your goals, the hours you dedicate to training will fluctuate and change.

I never recommend taking more than two classes per day of technique. If you take more than two classes per day, I recommend taking improvisation, dance composition, repertory classes, or somatics instead of more technique classes. By confining yourself to no more than

All Images: Anabella teaching at Peridance Center, NYC, 2017

two technique classes per day (or 3 hours of training), you can give 100% to both classes. If you take more, you will most likely find that you reach the limits of your focus and your concentration. Also, if you have rehearsals, you should be committing your full energy to the creative process.

There are times in our lives when we need to take class every day, but some days our bodies need to rest a little and see where other paths dance can lead us. The knowledge our bodies contain will always be there, but we have to guard against becoming weaker and stiffer.

What about flexibility? It has to do with relaxation of the muscles and ability to control your muscle tone and nervous system. Flexibility training requires that you are as relaxed as possible in order to be effective. Sometimes, if you take too many classes, you overwork your muscles and actually begin to lose flexibility. Classes are meant to prepare you for rehearsals and performances.

Six months after I had my first baby, I tried to come back to my training. It was extremely difficult, and I was taking only two classes per week. I realized it would be a very long journey. In my particular case, I couldn't dance when I was pregnant because I had a lot of problems with acid reflux, which meant every time I wasn't standing upright, I would burp or vomit. Lovely! After three months of that, I just had to stop. I didn't come back to dancing until a year later, when my son was about six months old.

Even then, coming back to training was hard. My body felt so different. I had lost strength, I had gained weight, my feet grew, my pelvis became wider, and my breasts grew too. My Italian genes showed up in a hurry. However, unexpectedly, I actually became more flexible after having a baby. I was at a crossroads, and I didn't know whether to keep dancing or not. It never crossed my mind to stop choreographing or directing my company though.

When I finally returned to a consistent routine of taking two classes per week, I realized I had to keep dancing because my body needed it. Taking class again was a kind of shock therapy for my body. It was like eating food again after having been hungry for so long. I had been letting my identity slip away, and now I was pulling it back in, like a deep, heavy anchor, hand by hand. I needed to keep dancing because my identity revolved around dance!

After having the baby, I was unhappy that the most I could take was two classes per week. Of course, the change from practicing every day for the many years before I was pregnant to just two classes per week made it difficult to maintain my psychological and emotional satisfaction. I thought to myself, "If I can't dance 100% again, why bother at all?" So, after three months, I stopped training completely because I wasn't satisfied with myself. Knowing my technique and style, anytime a company member couldn't perform, I personally could very easily replace that dancer. In this way, I kept dancing occasionally.

The biggest change for me was that after the baby arrived, I felt so much more human! I am convinced I've actually become a better dancer because of the weight of life that being a mother requires, both psychologically and physically. I feel more grounded. Yes, it was difficult after a long break, but I felt like I gained so much knowledge about my body as a woman from carrying and delivering the baby, nursing the baby, carrying the baby, etc., that I felt\much more powerful as a performer. It's one of life's peak experiences, like no other.

Young dancers can do five or 10 turns in a row, but you can see when someone has life experience or not. When you do a combination of movements, there is so much more to it than being young and able-bodied. When you see some of the older dancers in their 60s, 70s, or even 80s, their love, respect, and expertise blow me away. Thank God that technical progress in training gives us many more dancers who keep dancing until a later age. It's amazing and very moving.

After having my second child, I began training again and discovered that I have not lost any of my technique after all. It's like riding a bicycle, as they say. If you have a solid technique, it's always there. It just takes patience and generosity with yourself!

At the end of the day, how you train depends on your goals. Training isn't just taking classes and going to the gym. It's something beyond that. For me, even though I haven't taken regular dance classes these 10 years, I have been taking workshops on different topics, like theater, improvisation, and film—training I needed to reach my goals.

Sometimes you need different things from your training. Maybe you just need to read a book about dance and keep stretching, or maybe you need to take yoga or flamenco class! Try different art forms to open different realities that allow your body to be present. Dance is not just physical.

As a choreographer, I couldn't live without going to see dance performances or watching dance videos. If I stopped watching dance, I would have to stop being a choreographer. Going to see performances is an important part of my training!

We must continue to listen to ourselves because we are the only ones who know what we need—even when others try to tell you what's "right" for you. A large part of training is learning to listen to yourself. Think about what you want to do, and the proper path of training will become clear. Also, you must speak with your mentors for guidance.

I am a performer, a choreographer, a writer, and a teacher. I think about what I need to practice or learn to attain balance and harmony within myself. As a teacher, I've tried many techniques—dance related and not dance related—so I feel I have the tools and information I need to tell my students what resources can help them on their journeys.

Pain & Pleasure

As dancers and performers, sometimes we feel like sadomasochists. We seem to enjoy pain, thinking "more pain, more work, better muscles, better dancing." Through dance training, however, we can realize that we don't need to suffer. Of course we need to work hard, but hard work doesn't have to mean pain or, worse yet, injuries.

If I have an injury in my knee, why would I keep overworking it? As dancers or performers, we should learn to incorporate pauses into our practice and learn how to listen to and respect the rhythm of our bodies. If we have consistent pain, we must take a moment to deal with that pain. Think about a long-term plan. Think about the future.

Identify the pain: What kind of pain is it? What is the degree of pain on a scale of 1-10? If you notice that you have pain in your knee but have a show in a few days, first assess the pain, and then think about the long-term plan for your career to decide whether to perform or not.

The fact is that to be a dancer or performer you will deal with pain—psychological, physical, and emotional. However, a lot of that pain is avoidable.

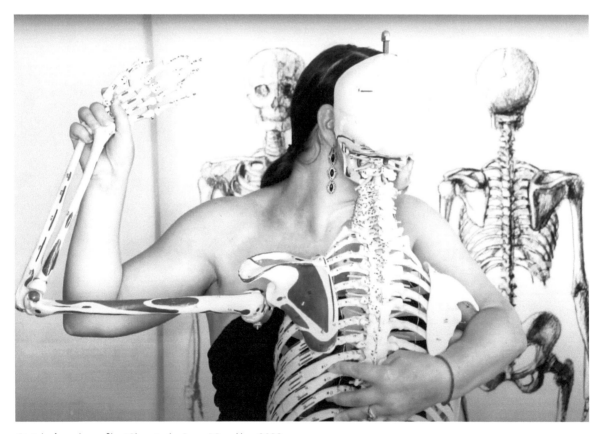

Outtake from dance film "Close to the Bone," Brooklyn, 2022

157

In the 1990s, when I was training in Argentina, more than half of the dancers I trained with suffered from bulimia or anorexia. That was unnecessary pain. During that time, I started to unnecessarily overuse and exploit my body. I then felt pain in certain areas of my body, but I did not want to listen to my body. I focused on pain instead of opening my entire body to understanding why the pain was there. It was like going to work with a toothache. The toothache will always eventually win the battle, and it will be all you can think about.

Here in the United States, I hear the phrase, "No pain no gain," but what does this mean? Yes, it can bring you to another level of consciousness, but when pain blocks you or confuses you, it is useless to just focus on the pain.

I was bulimic in my youth and overcame this with the help of my family. I decided that I would focus on the pleasure that my body gave me by elevating my feelings of joy, fullness, and satisfaction after training and performing. I focused on the pleasure of creating, on bodily expression, and on sharing the joy of self-care and self-discovery through teaching and performing.

Outtake from dance film "Out of the Folds of Women," Brooklyn, 2020

Outtake from dance film "Out of the Folds of Women," Brooklyn, 2020

What Kind of Performer Are You?

In creating and directing several dance companies in Argentina, Italy, and the United States all these years, I've needed different kinds of performers at different times for different projects. There are many different types of performers. For example, sometimes I need a dancer who just follows instructions, and sometimes I need a creative performer.

It is important that you identify which type of performer you are. This will help you find which companies you want to work with since the type of performer a company looks for is closely tied to how a choreographer works.

Do you enjoy following directions? Do you feel more secure when you work in a company with a set repertory, or do you prefer to share your creative points of view during the process? Do you have a deep need for your own voice to be heard, or do you find fulfillment in being a vessel or medium in service of another artist's idea? As a dance artist, I need to share my own points of view. Is that true for you too?

Both types of performer can be creative, but working with a repertory company is different from working with a company that is building new choreography. For example, let's say you are in a company that re-creates classics from their repertory. You might be asked to participate in an adaptation of *Giselle* set in the 1970s, in the middle of the dictatorial government in Argentina! You'll need to research and adapt to the style and historical context. You will use your creativity in the re-interpretation of the piece.

When you work with an innovative choreographer or director who is building a new repertory, you may not know exactly what, why, where, and how the creation will turn out. The piece will be built through improvisation and exploration. Obviously, this is creative as well. You will be part of the creative team, and you can inspire the team in creating something new.

By exploring different types of projects you can discover which one(s) you feel most comfortable with. Perhaps you will feel comfortable with all of it! Also keep in mind that different types of auditions will guide you along a path to a variety of artistic projects. Working with different companies at the beginning of your career will help you to know your preferences.

I was always closely aligned with improvisation and experimental works, so I was never interested in being in a repertory company, although I was trained and performed in the ballet and modern dance repertory. This training taught me the many ways I could later approach my own choreography.

I have found that opportunities present themselves when you are ready to take them. In the early 2000s, I interviewed the modern dancer and master teacher Betty Jones, who taught me Limón technique and repertory. She told me, "You open the door to yourself when you are ready. Wait and see." **Always remain in communication with yourself, and when you are ready, you will open the door.**

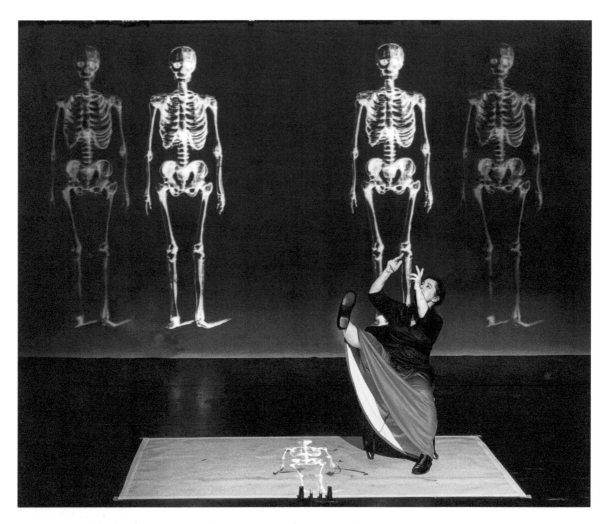

"Listen to Your Mother" performance at La Mama Moves Festival, NYC, 2024

To Continue or Quit, That Is the Question

In my life, I've stopped my training as a performer a few times. The first time I was 18 years old and had injured my Achilles tendon very badly. It took me six months to recover. It was hard because I felt I was in my technical prime. I learned a lot about how to take care of my body. The silver lining of the recovery process was that I came to deeply understand how my body and my mind work, as well as how far I can push them in performance. I learned about my mental limits too! The second time I stopped my training was when I moved from the United States to Italy. Working as a choreographer and teacher, I didn't have time to train my body regularly. I was also performing two or three times a week, and it was very hard for me to keep in good enough dance shape for the type of performing I was doing at the time. The third time I stopped was when I had my first baby. Since then, my training has changed radically.

It is hard for a dedicated dancer to stop training, and it often brings depression and anxiety. There was a time when I thought that if I didn't take class everyday, giving 100%, it wasn't worth it. It was all or nothing, and I made dance my identity without reservation. Dancers or performers who stop training often lose self-esteem because dance and performance are intimately connected to their identities and self-worth. Maintaining a consistent training schedule becomes a very strong habit for the body and mind. Dance and performance training becomes as important as daily bread. As I discuss starting on page 66 in Chapter 7, dance and performance is a way of life for those who choose it.

We dancers and performers have high standards, and if we don't attain those standards, we get down on ourselves. This can easily feed an unhealthy attitude because if you focus on your shortcomings or failures, your dissatisfaction can make you quit. Most of the hurdles to long-term training and performing are psychological, although of course there are physical factors if you overwork yourself.

Over time, I gradually realized that I didn't need to be perfect. This took time because as traditional ballet dancers, perfection was expected of us from day one. Perfect lines, perfect execution, 100% accuracy. But I learned to take care of myself, be patient, and accept what I could do and what I could not. I became my own best friend!

So when do you stop dancing or performing? It's up to each individual when and whether to make this decision. It depends on what makes sense for you as a unique human being.

After my Achilles tendon injury, I knew I would never return to the training I undertook when I was 18, but I wasn't going to stop dancing or lower my standards of perfection as a goal. What's important is that I was able to accept that perfection is truly unattainable and fictional. The pursuit of an ideal is admirable, but basing your self-worth on achieving perfection is not realistic. What is right for me will necessarily be different from what is right for others.

In the end, life makes you set your priorities and define your approach to being a dancer or performer. As a mother, educator, and artist, my priority now is to be healthy and in tune with my own values.

Changes are difficult in any career, but especially in the performing arts. Only you have the power to decide to keep going or to quit. Sometimes the body says stop, but the mind keeps dancing. My advice is to continue dancing in other ways, perhaps by writing, teaching, or choreographing.

Which choice you make depends a lot on your attitude, but also on your support system. Are you feeling supported, and by whom? Identify who you rely on, who you can talk to about this and other important decisions. Is it your family, your partner, your friends, colleagues, mentors, etc.? When you feel your support system cheering you on, everything is easier. Work on making the decision that makes the most sense to you. **Don't be alone on this journey. Surround yourself with people who love and respect you and your career.**

Outtake from dance film "Out of the Folds of Women," Brooklyn, 2020

Value of Your Career as a Dancer

When someone asks you what you do for a living and you say, "I'm a dancer," or "I am a performer," some people think that you are a bohemian, just having fun, pursuing dance or performance as a superficial hobby. No matter what country or culture you come from, a dance career is unfortunately often considered low class, and makes you fear or even feel like you are not a serious person. This misunderstanding makes me deeply sad, and says a lot about the role of art and performance in many people's lives. I believe artists, dancers, and performers are a necessary part of our society.

When you become an artist, dancer, or performer, you acquire certain skills that are important for life as a whole. You develop a sense of ethics, a sense of life, a sense of style, a sense of creativity, a sense of beauty, and a sense of responsibility to yourself, others, and your community. You learn to improvise, how to quickly identify problems and quickly find solutions, how to be a nerd, how to drive a car better. I think it's the best education a child can have. That's why I've enrolled my children in dance classes.

The sense of discipline you gain through dance class is very important in life. The sense of personal responsibility that you are required to have when you go to dance class is vital. The 90 minutes you spend in class not speaking, taking direction, practicing how to manage your body, how to concentrate, and how to focus are vital.

The arts in general provide a strong education. In some ways, dance is much healthier than sports because dance also cultivates a sensibility for others and for yourself that is important.

I feel that people don't understand that value. Everyone loves to see a performance, but nobody wants to pay. So one response to this has been choreographers opening rehearsals to the public, showing them what dance is so they can realize how difficult it is. Everybody loves to see a dancer warming up, for example. People start to have some respect for dance in this way.

"Listen to Your Mother" performance at La Mama Moves Festival, NYC, 2024

Questioning Yourself and the System

To grow and develop as an artist, dancer, or performer you must question yourself. I cannot over-emphasize its importance. However, there can indeed be a danger in questioning too much. It can become unhealthy and distracting. How can you find a balance?

What that balance is for you depends, in part, on your intuition. Intuition is like an internal compass. If you don't know how to listen, it will stop your forward progress and you'll become frozen. Listen to your quiet inner questions, or you may lose your inner compass.

At some point in my career my questions became less internal, and I started to ask questions about external issues. Age and life experience typically give you greater confidence to amplify your questions.

What does the word "success" mean to you? For me, success doesn't mean being rich and famous. For me, success is freedom of expression. It is being able to work in my chosen career and be paid fairly for it. Success means that I can do what I want to do, including being able to take risks.

One piece of advice: When questioning what you do and why you do it is so challenging that your system cannot absorb anything else, it is helpful to stop and focus on the positive aspects of your career and decisions. You need to realize that sometimes you must be your own support system, and it is important to be constructive and celebrate your achievements and victories, however small they may seem.

Both Images: Outtake from dance film "The Night That You Stopped Acting/ La Noche que dejaste de Actuar," Brooklyn, 2020

Also, just because others' external achievements are championed by popular culture, you must give yourself the freedom to question whether those achievements really resonate with you. Sometimes we look at flowers and think, "Oh, these flowers are so beautiful," and then realize the flowers are plastic. Sometimes the plastic flowers look even more beautiful and perfect than natural flowers, but they are not real! Do you really appreciate that perfection, or do you prefer the real but imperfect thing, or did realizing the flowers are fake interest you more?

Sometimes it worries me that in the field of dance, there is not enough internal or external questioning. For more on this topic, I invite you to read an article I wrote on my blog in 2014, titled "Am I going to get a job? It's highly unlikely: Masters in Dance vs Professional Experience."
https://anabellalenzu.wordpress.com/2014/10/28/am-i-going-to-get-a-job-its-highly-unlike/

In the article, I sought a variety of other opinions to illuminate different aspects of this question, so I invited a few important personalities in the dance world to share their thoughts, including: Silvana Cardell from Georgian Court University, New Jersey; James Martin from NYU/Tisch; Amy Larimer from Lehman College/CUNY; Sara Rudner from Sarah Lawrence; Tanya Calamoneri, Ph.D. in dance; and Elizabeth Keen from Juilliard School. In short, titles are titles, papers are papers, but if you truly know your field, it doesn't matter what title you have or paper you've published. In the United States, artists feel obligated to pay at least $40,000 per year to enroll in a master's-level dance degree program because they need to find stability, a home, time to research, and the resources to learn the tools needed to explore, develop, and create their art and craft. Enrolling in a master's program is a luxury that not everyone can afford. Do we need to participate in this system to be valued in this society?

What happens to the formation of dancers around the world? Is college the place where an artist develops? Is it in the small academies, open studios, small companies, or large dance groups? Dancers, teachers, and choreographers travel the world to learn, practice, and experiment, and they don't always gravitate to the universities.

However, somehow we have all agreed on the system of higher education to give the stamp of authority. I do not have the answer to this problem, but I am convinced that it's important to ask such questions. Accepting things without questioning brings us nothing but mediocrity. That is why we need to question the system.

I invite you to take action and find solutions because all of us are making dance history. All of us are part of this community. Deep care is the answer. I want to be part of a system that values sacrifice, work, commitment. That is why I keep going, and that is why I write about it.

Mentors

What does the word mentor mean in our Western culture? According to Merriam-Webster, a mentor is a "trusted counselor or guide … [a] tutor, coach." To "mentor" is "to teach or guide usually individually in a special subject or for a particular purpose." We use the word for someone who has a positive, guiding influence on another person's life.

Not every dance teacher can or wants to be a mentor because it's a mutual decision of total generosity between mentor and mentee. Finding the right mentor is like finding the right partner. It's complicated! Being a mentor is essentially about being a role model in all aspects—professionally, artistically, ethically—which implies responsibility and deep care.

As a Latina artist living and working in New York City, I have often reflected on my past and my future and what it means to be a mentor in these times. Being a mentor is not just being a source of inspiration, much less a reference on a job application. It is about committing to deep dialogue, sometimes intense and difficult.

What is the difference between teaching and mentoring?

- On one hand, teaching is about knowledge. The teacher shares their knowledge through instruction and explanation. In the traditional sense, teaching involves formal lessons on a subject, often including a detailed lesson plan and methods of assessment.
- By contrast, mentoring is about experience. It is more informal and relational. A mentor acts as an advisor, sharing lessons learned from their lived experience. There's more sharing as mentors strive to help their mentees grow into peers.

Why do we need mentors in our artistic lives? Young artists are sometimes lost and disoriented. It's not uncommon to bounce between feeling wildly insecure and being a devilish rebel. Growing into the life of an artist is difficult but very rewarding! Mentors aid in navigating one's fear of failure, eliminating distractions, and locating resources while often helping to contend with a poor emotional, economical, or psychological support system. **Mentors are like beacons. They can help reorient you, helping you find your inner strength and your artistic underpinnings or "ancestors."**

When I am teaching (especially dance criticism or dance history), I often find that many people are unfamiliar with important and influential dancers, teachers, or choreographers who came before them, and they are not curious at all about learning about these people. They exhibit a kind of arrogant ignorance, not understanding that although they believe they are creating something new, they are actually repeating something that was first done decades ago. Of course, we cannot know everything, but it is a waste of energy and it shows ignorance to do something that's already a part of the shared dance legacy. Dance education is about honoring the past, celebrating diversity, and doing research in order to move ahead and push the boundaries of our field.

I feel that we need to be in dialogue with our artistic ancestors so we can make true progress and grow as artists and human beings. The old adage is true: You have to know where you've been in order to know where you are going. Mentors help you in that journey. Sometimes we need to rebel against our ancestors and disagree with our mentors, and that's also part of growing for some!

Most of my mentors were international visual artists, writers, regisseurs, theater directors, and choreographers. Why? As a curious artist, I needed to know what happened behind the scenes in different genres. How could I "make it" as an artist in a world where knowledge was so scarce? I needed to understand the artist and the person behind each of my mentors to find out who I was.

There is an important distinction to be made between mentors and the many inspirational artists I never met in person. Being involved with different art forms and disciplines has given me a broader and deeper perspective to understand the possibilities and limitations of my own artistic choices.

My first mentor was the Argentinean sculptor Rafael Martin (1935-2018). I studied sculpture with him during 1995-1999 in Bahia Blanca, Argentina. Guy Ariel Kruh (born in 1953), a French semiologist and regisseur, was my second mentor; I studied semiology of theater and the Delsart system with him.

My first choreographic mentor was the American dancer and teacher Jim May. Under his wing, I learned to be even more acute in my artistic choices in the dance field. When I moved back to the U.S. in 2005, I took classes with him when he was the artistic director of the Anna Sokolow Dance project, but after two months I just quit. Jim could not understand why I did not come to class. It was not because I did not like the class or because of the technique. I just felt that his teaching was having too strong an influence on my movement vocabulary, and every time I would begin my own choreography, I was using Anna's choreographic approach. I needed to create some distance, not personally but artistically. I needed space to explore who I was.

In 2007, Jim asked me to choreograph for the Anna Sokolow Theater Ensemble, Of course, I said yes, as it was a tremendous honor. It was thrilling to recombine my own voice with Jim and Anna's technique and artistry. I was already on another path, finding my own way.

I am afraid that some students can never find their own voices because they remain under the influence of a certain style, teacher, or academy. Some dancers need to hold onto their traditions because they feel their function (or mission?) is to keep that tradition going and pass it on to the next generation.

Other dancers and choreographers feel compelled to find their own voices, and that was my path. It was painful to stop my classes in Sokolow technique with Jim May. I simultaneously missed those classes and recognized that I wasn't being myself. I was molding myself to the people and choreographers I trained with.

It is okay to cite a dance ancestor in your choreography, fully aware that the work was created by someone else but you wish to echo it or pay homage to it in your work. The problem arises when you are unaware of these influences or are unaware that you are actually using their work in your own.

Do carry on a dialogue with your artistic ancestors, but don't be reluctant to argue with them—even if you agree and admire them—in order to find your own voice, your own attitude. Of course, part of who you are will be influenced by your forebears, but you have the opportunity to develop an even more deeply authentic theory, and you might actually take the exact opposite path.

Outtake from dance film "Lucky Star," Brooklyn, 2021

166

Whatever the case, it is very important that you look for mentors. Mentors will typically not come to you. Instead, you as an artist need to get closer to what you like. Get close to the fire. Allow a mentor to "infect" you with the knowledge they have to offer. Maybe it will just be for a short period of time and you move on. Most mentors will understand that progression because they have had these experiences. I sometimes tell students, "I love that you come to my class, but don't stay in my class forever. You need to move on and learn other things."

It is your responsibility as a teacher and mentor to generously give freedom to your students. You want them to be independent, not dependent on you. You want them to open their wings, to find their own artistic voices. As a mentor, part of my job is to help them to think for themselves because, as Bell Hooks said, "Education is the practice of freedom."

Mentor and mentee choose each other. Sometimes I've chosen a mentor and they did not choose me. In some ways it's like a romantic relationship: one person initiates and one pursues the other. There's a mutual agreement, and experience and knowledge are transmitted. One reason it is important to have mentors is that we benefit from having artistic, spiritual, and ethical dialogues. **A good mentor is an eternal support, a point of reference.**

Once, I thought I found my true mentor, one of my ballet teachers in Argentina. I loved her. I even copied her attitudes and gestures. She was great. She was a mother of two children and also had a successful international career as a dancer. She was elegant, very professional. I just loved her—that is, until I started to choreograph. I was 16 years old, and I began to choreograph one piece that was supposed to be performed for a festival. I invited her to

Anabella teaching "My Body, My Country" body mapping workshop at Columbia University, NYC, 2019

167

Both Images: "Listen to Your Mother" performance at La Mama Moves Festival, NYC, 2024

one of my rehearsals, and she did not like what she saw. She said, "This is not a democratic system. If you want to perform this piece for the festival, I will not allow you to perform in my company anymore."

This was a very painful experience because I admired this woman enormously. But then I realized that her reaction came out of jealousy as I began to spread my wings. So even though I still admired her greatly, I never returned to her classes or her company. I stopped dancing for her. I felt that she was not the right mentor for me because she did not encourage me to find my own voice as a choreographer. I am very thankful for all the technical lessons and insights she gave me, but not the artistic or professional aspects. The jealousy she expressed, and her competitive impulses governed what she said, and that drove us apart.

Finding a mentor that's right for you is about seeing them as a kind of mirror of your future self. Are you projecting yourself onto them or idealizing your future self? Either is possible, but being with the right mentor will help you embrace who you really are and bloom into your potential. Many of my mentees over the years have told me that they learn simultaneously how to be an artist and a woman by seeing themselves reflected in my daily choices as both artist and mother.

Back in June 2020, in the midst of the Covid-19 pandemic, after hearing the needs of my international dance community, students, and dancers, who sought personal coaching and mentoring, I created two online programs: Online Choreographic Mentorship Workshops and the 1-ON-1 Choreographic Mentorship. Many students wanted not only to receive encouragement and to improve technically and artistically during this difficult and isolating time, but also to be present in an online hub/virtual space and spend high-quality time in a place where artists could meet, connect, exchange ideas, and collaborate.

The pandemic underscored that I must always be prepared to adapt, grow, and think "outside the box"! It was refreshing for me to be able to teach online, which led me to create new methodologies. Since I began teaching online in March 2020, I have observed students developing their focus, commitment, and enthusiasm, but not all students feel engaged while studying online. Being so isolated made some of them feel disconnected from their own bodies and lost. That's why I have found myself needing to change my online practice. Depending on the content, I either shorten class time or meet just once a week for a longer period to avoid ZOOM fatigue.

Adapting the class rhythm, time administration, content, and sources of inspiration helps keep students engaged. I share with them articles, readings, and videos to explore on their own time, research, and study, so through critical thinking, I guide them into dialogue and discussions about the topics and thereby empower students, create community, and enjoy camaraderie. I've found that during the pandemic, we shared our vulnerability, our private spaces, and our art in a deeper way!

Why do I make myself available as a mentor? When you love what you do so much, you want to share it. Also, because I received so much love and care as a mentee, I feel a responsibility to "pay it forward" to the next generation of dancers, choreographers, and teachers. I want to make a better future for everyone and help make a better community. Dance, for me, is the union of a person with her interior. It is a communion with yourself, with others, with the environment, and with life.

PART III
TEACHER RESOURCES

"My Body, My Country," Photographic Exhibition at Spoke the Hub, 2024

PEDAGOGY III
INSTRUCTOR: ANABELLA LENZU

Course Goals

Objectives
- To offer methodological tools of analysis about how to teach, organize, and create a teaching plan
- To promote artistic education to enhance the social and cultural community
- To preserve and develop artistic social values
- To contribute to the development of the socio-cultural community
- To offer knowledge, promote investigation, and increase creative ability
- To be conscious that dance is a cultural, technical, pedagogical, and aesthetic phenomenon
- To unite dancer, student, professor, and choreographer in open discussion
- To integrate mind and heart
- To solve internal problems within specialized pedagogies
- To generate a reflective space for dialogue where each participant's thoughts and experiences are respected
- Write a pedagogical statement, teaching philosophy, and 10-year teaching development plan
- Identify NYC resources for dance research and development

Why?
- Because dance must be respected and understood not as a diversion or pastime but, rather, as one of our most beautiful and complex arts in which body, mind, and creative spirit are continuously rendered and exposed
- Because it should be our duty to help professionals, amateurs, and students in dance resolve problems and thereby raise the socio-cultural level all while respecting our differences and experiences
- Because all techniques and styles imply a corresponding methodology and pedagogy
- Because we need a humanistic approach to art and dance education
- Because we need continuing education to improve ourselves and participate creatively in society and in the culture in which we live
- Because education should be a preparation for living and dance is a profound exploration of life.
- Because we must improve how we teach dance as a theoretical and practical discipline
- Because we need to continue taking courses to improve ourselves and our specialization

Student Will Be Taught

Module I: Education
Definition of concepts: learning, education, instruction, pedagogy, didactic, methodology
Basic problems of teachers of dance
Measuring a school's success
Education
Self education and training
Self-discipline
Communication
Emotions and learning
Programs and planning
Strategy, tactics, logistics
Aesthetics and ethical values
Stimuli and motivation
Development: emotive or affective, intellectual, physical, perceptual, social, aesthetic

Practical Work
- Define and analyze conceptually: purpose/goals, pedagogical orientation, and learning processes in the teaching of dance
- Plan a class

Module II: Creativity

Definition of concepts: imagination and creativity
History of creativity
Stages: prescientific, pre-experimental, experimental
Creative processes; development and encouragement of creativity
Creativity in childhood; creativity in adolescence
Factors and inhibitors of creativity
Creative group, creative students, creative masters

Module III: What Is Art?

Art as an important element of the company
The formative principle of art
Art as a means of interpretation of development
Meaning of arts in education
Dance making/composition: role of the choreographer; relationship of music and dance
Art in elementary school

Module IV. The Art of Dance

Key aspects of the art of dance
Dance as an art form
The importance of artistic products
Expression of the body
Dance and its relation to other arts; artistic phenomena; artistic values
Discovering a student's skills
Why do we move? The experience of the body
Mental and physical health

Module V: Student, Teacher, Institution, Parents

Search one's identity to delineate the professional identity
The profile of the student
Relationship between student, teacher, and parents
Roles
Times and stages: classes through the ages; dance for children, adolescents, adults
Training
Dance therapy
Dance as a hobby
Dance as a profession
Amateur vs. professional
The role of the school/institution/academy
Classes/workshops/master classes/intensives
Studies and responsibilities
Duties and obligations of teachers and students

Required Books

Teaching and Learning Dance Through Meaningful Gestures by Anabella Lenzu is available on both Kindle and hard copy on Amazon.
Unveiling Motion and Emotion by Anabella Lenzu is available on both Kindle and hard copy on Amazon.
Teaching to Transgress by Bell Hooks.

Recommended Books

Education for Critical Consciousness by Paulo Freire
Teaching Critical Thinking by Bell Hooks
Choreographing Empathy by Susan Lee Foster
The Art of Making Dances by Doris Humphrey
Dancers Talking Dance by Larry Lavender
How to Look at Dance by Walter Terry
Choreography Observed by Jack Anderson
The Modern Dance by John Martin
Development of Creative Ability by Victor Lowenfeld and Brittain W. Lambert

Both Images: Anabella teaching at Heifetz Institute, VA, 2023

BALLET PRINCIPLES III
PROFESSOR: ANABELLA LENZU

Course Description

The study, experience, and analysis of fundamental ballet principles and techniques of barre, adagio, and petite and grand allegro.

Find your inner strength. Dance with joy. Develop alignment and ballet technique. Explore and learn how to efficiently use your body and your energy in a healthy way as an instrument of your expression. Increase flexibility and strength and acquire muscular awareness to prevent injuries. Overcome physical difficulties, incorrect posture, or inflexibility.

The focus of this class is to further develop and deepen an understanding of the principles of ballet practices. This class will help you develop skills basic to all movement studies, such as dynamic alignment through coordination and integration of the neuro/skeletal/muscular system, strength, balance, and spatial and rhythmic awareness.

At all levels, DNC 203 Ballet Principles III will guide students in creative and expressive freedom by enhancing the qualities of ease, grace, musicality, and symmetry that define the form. To this end, we will explore alignment with an emphasis on anatomical principles and on the appropriate neuromuscular effort needed to dance with optimal integration of every aspect of the individual body, mind, and spirit.

Learning Objectives

- To learn, develop, and understand the fundamentals of ballet technique
- To have a clear knowledge of and ability to perform the ballet movement vocabulary at the barre and center
- To be familiar with the most common ballet terminology
- To know the names of major bones and muscles
- To understand alignment principles and be able to apply them to different ballet movement vocabulary
- To perform choreography before an audience on stage and demonstrate techniques and skills learned in class

Class Description for Ballet

1. **Warm-up.** Each class starts with warm-up exercises (standing or floor) to increase flexibility and strength and to develop muscular awareness to prevent injuries.
2. **Barre à Terre (Floor Work):** To learn, develop, and understand the vocabulary of ballet technique. Explore the use of space, dynamic coordination, and body control of energy. We compare how exercises and alignment of the body affect the upright position and the different effects of gravity on the dancer.
3. **Barre:** To learn, develop, and understand the vocabulary of ballet technique. Develop alignment and an understanding of the principle of projection of energy. Study breath control to understand how it affects movement. Study body control and spatial awareness.
4. **Center:** Balance exercises and change of weight.
5. **Diagonal:** Use movement phrases to study specific technical aspects, such as pirouettes, jumps, change of focus/space/direction/velocity/flow of energy.

A great deal of emphasis will be on consciously working on ballet technique to overcome physical difficulties, such as incorrect posture or inflexibility. Focus will be on exploring and projecting energy to the infinite.

Alignment and muscular awareness will be emphasized as injury prevention.

Both Images: Fiamma Lenzu-Carroll performing "Listen to Your Mother" at La Mama Moves Festival, NYC, 2024

ONLINE VIDEO LIBRARY:
ANATOMY & DANCE

Among other things, I find YouTube to be a great resource for expanding my knowledge about dance and learning about other artists. As a choreographer and professor of dance history, dance criticism, and anatomy, I created a library on my page so that dancers can view and analyze historical and contemporary dance pieces.

I created 150 playlists (with approximately 2,000 videos) organized by historical period and choreographer, as well as 3D animated videos of anatomy.

Please SUBSCRIBE to my YouTube page in order to receive updates to the online video library. **https://www.youtube.com/user/AnabellaLenzu**

Top: Anabella & journalist Celia Ipiotis filming in Greenpoint, Brooklyn, 2021
Bottom: Anabella teaching online, 2021

USEFUL DANCE METAPHORS

A few years ago, I sent out a call on social media to some of my students around the world, asking them to send me phrases or expressions they remembered me saying while studying with me. Many of them transported me back to a certain time in my life, and to my surprise, I had completely forgotten about some of the things I'd said.

When I'm teaching, I routinely come up with spontaneous imagery and metaphors in an attempt to help dancers and performers achieve their maximum potential, or simply to give them an alternate approach to understanding the principles of training. It was interesting to hear from my old students and find out which off-the-cuff remarks live on in their memories.

If you have ever taken one of my classes, maybe some of these phrases will sound familiar, but if not, perhaps one or two will help you open a door to self-knowledge. Enjoy them!

"Please do your plies like pressing a soft marshmallow" and **"Your plies are like a soft cake, not like an old bagel!"**
– Garrett

"You always use the image of motorcycle handles to explain activation of the abductor muscles!"
– John Thacker

"Send the energy to specific locations and geographical points."

"Project your energy from Union Square to Central Park! From Brooklyn to New Jersey!"

"Make your hands sing with energy."

"Being in balance is not being still. Balance is active. It is continuous motion."

"Rotate your hands from the middle fingers—like drilling."

"Breathe and expand the intercostal muscles on the back of your ribs! Breathe into the back ribs!"
– Patricia (About Projection of Energy into Space)

"Vroooom vrooooom! Turnout!"

"Open your face! Open your forehead!"

["That actually made me feel my face and be more aware of my presence in the room."]
– Allyson Reanne Trunzer

"The body is never static. Energy always flows and comes out through our extremities. Movement is energy. It is always present. It never ceases to exist. Think about it as continuous and infinite."

"Control gives freedom."
– Claudia Berea Ceceña

"The body is like a puzzle and each piece has to be in its place so we can achieve our position in order to dance."

"You don't need strength to turn. Just rise and elevate yourself!"
– Maria Noelia Massarella

"How do you see or perceive yourself from inside? And from outside?"
– Lindsay Marie Schaefer

"Please take out the words 'I can't' from your vocabulary!"

"Who are you? Show me this when you dance!"

– Mari Laura Lavigna

"Imagine a string from the center of the head that passes through the center of the body and exits from the pee-pee hole. Feel the opposition of the string up and down."

"This opposition is like the tension on the strings of an instrument. Too much tension and it will break: If there is not enough opposition, you will collapse. Find the middle point so the sound and the movement emerge!"

– Julieta Zaragoza

"Please never say 'I can't'! Say 'I will try'!"

– Gullermina Menguele

"Always be aware of your kinesphere as you dance or perform!"

– Darrian O'Reilly

"Performance is like kissing your new boyfriend or girlfriend while your old boyfriend or girlfriend is watching you. You feel your lips, your tongue, your saliva, but you are provoking your old boyfriend or girlfriend at the same time."

– Liz Gorgas

"Is it not enough to act as if we were experiencing an emotion such as anger or pretend as if we were screaming. We needed to connect with the emotion and let the body translate it into a real vibration we share with the audience."

"It wasn't enough to feel the emotion or the gesture either. We needed to work to communicate it for the rest to witness."

– Katie Clancy

"Have the image in mind when you are falling to sleep and your eyelids are heavy and falling, when the body is giving up. This is the sensation of fall and recovery!"

– Martina Pantani (Regarding the modern dance principle of fall and recovery from Doris Humphrey)

"Move your arms energetically from your spine! Like devils' or angels' wings from your dorsal muscles."

– Martina Pantani

"Kick your balls!"

– Jake Tyler Marks (About the pas de chat step)

"When you lie down on the floor, feel flat like a pancake, like a sticker, like a steak on the grill."

– Ryan Moroney

"Spread your toes like the roots of a tree in the ground."

– Brianna Brice

"Please don't do the feet bananas!!!"

– Tanishia

"Enjoy it like a dark chocolate melting in your mouth."

– Fiamma

Both Images: Anabella teaching at Peridance Center, NYC, 2024

ILLUSTRATIONS OF EXERCISES
Illustrations by Rathi Varma

ABC Series

Teaching and Learning Dance through Meaningful Gestures
by Anabella Lenzu

Against Barre or Wall

Teaching and Learning Dance through Meaningful Gestures
by Anabella Lenzu

Against Barre or Wall

Teaching and Learning Dance through Meaningful Gestures
by Anabella Lenzu

Arm Exercises

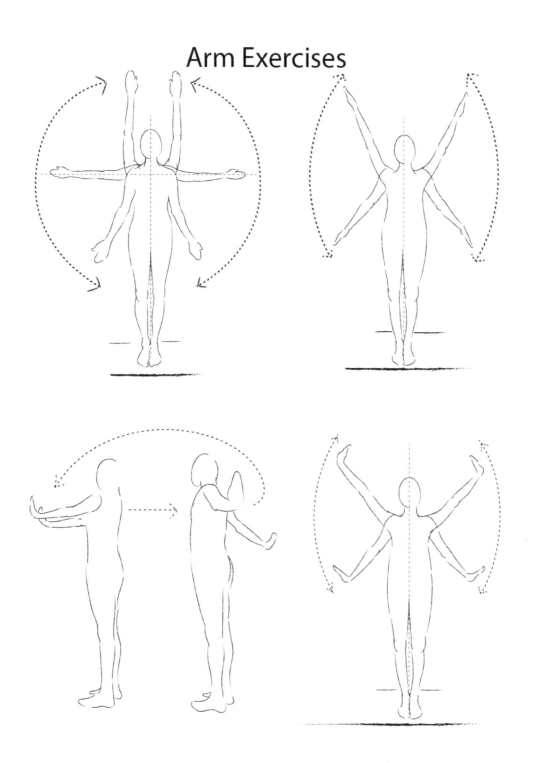

Teaching and Learning Dance through Meaningful Gestures
by Anabella Lenzu

Theraband Exercises

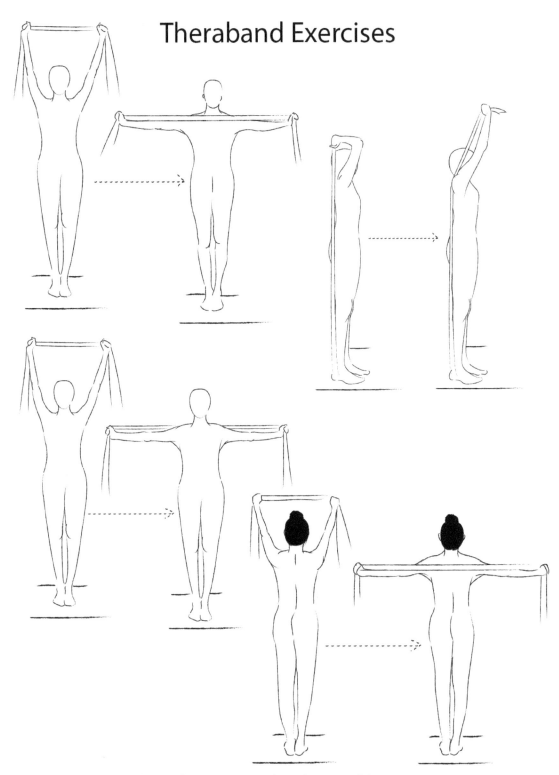

Teaching and Learning Dance through Meaningful Gestures
by Anabella Lenzu

186

Theraband Exercises

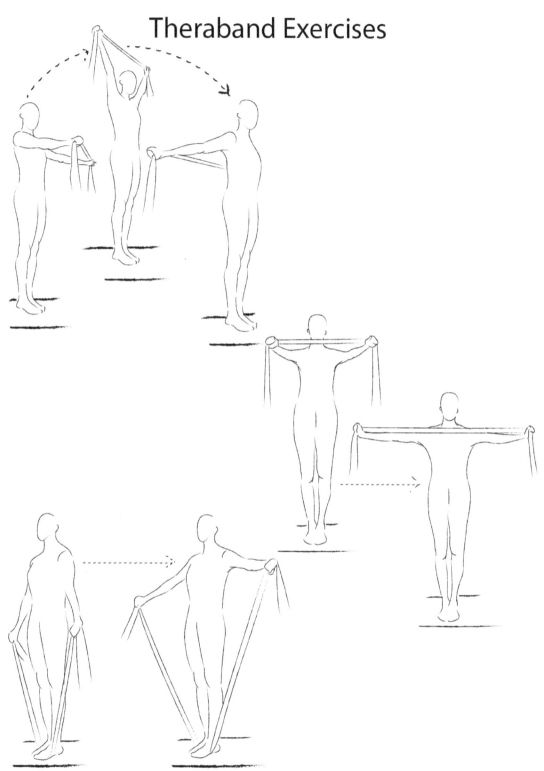

Teaching and Learning Dance through Meaningful Gestures
by Anabella Lenzu

AUTHOR BIOGRAPHY

Exhibition of Anabella's photographs at the premiere of "Listen to Your Mother" at La Mama Downstairs Theater, NYC, 2024

Originally from Argentina, Anabella Lenzu is a dancer, choreographer, scholar, and educator with over 30 years of experience working in Argentina, Chile, Italy, and the United States.

Lenzu directs her own company, Anabella Lenzu/DanceDrama, which since 2006 has created 15 choreographic works that have been given in 400 performances at 100 venues, presenting thought-provoking and historically conscious dance-theater in NYC.

As a choreographer, Anabella has received commissions from all over the world and by many companies and other entities for dance works, opera, television programs, theater productions. Lenzu has produced and directed several award-winning short dance films and has screened her work in over 200 festivals both nationally and internationally, including Argentina, Bolivia, Brazil, Canada, Cyprus, France, Germany, Greece, India, Indonesia, Ireland, Italy, Kenya, London, Mexico, Norway, Poland, Portugal, Romania, Serbia, Spain, Switzerland, United Kingdom, United States, and Venezuela.

Anabella's work has been presented at La Mama, Baryshnikov Arts Center, Movement Research at Judson Church, Draftworks at DanceSpace project/St. Mark's Church, 92nd Street Y, HERE Arts Center, Abrons Arts Center, DUO Multicultural Arts Center, Queens Museum, Bronx Museum, Gibney Dance, Center for Performance Research, Triskelion, Chez Bushwick, Roulette, Chashama, Dixon Place, Sheen Center, the Consulate of Argentina in New York City, NYU/Casa Zerilli Marimo, University Settlement, Baruch Performing Arts Center, BAAD, Snug Harbor Cultural Center, Instituto Cervantes, 3LD Center for Art & Technology, Kumble Theater/Long Island University, and at many other venues. She has received grants from New York State Council of the Arts, Brooklyn Arts Council, Harkness Foundation for Dance, Puffin Foundation, Rockefeller Brothers Fund, Foundation for Contemporary Arts Emergency Grant, Edwards Foundation, Vermont Community Foundation, and the Independent Community Foundation.

Lenzu was awarded her MFA in Fine Arts (concentration in Choreography) from Wilson College, Pennsylvania. Classically trained at the renowned Teatro Colòn in Buenos Aires, Argentina, Lenzu studied the modern dance techniques of Humphrey/Limón and Martha Graham in New York. Her studies of tango and the folk dances of Argentina, Spain, and Italy, further inform her work.

Lenzu founded her own dance school, L'Atelier Centro Creativo de Danza, in 1994 in Bahia Blanca, Argentina, and has been an educator for over 30 years, teaching in more than 50 institutions, including universities, professional dance studios, companies, festivals, and symposiums in the United States, Canada, Ireland, Egypt, Australia, Panamá, Mexico, Argentina, Brazil, Chile, England, and Italy.

Anabella received the National Award for Outstanding Leadership in the Independent Sector by National Dance Education Organization in 2023, having been awarded the Innovative Dance Educator Award by New York State Dance Education Association in 2022 to acknowledge her work as a dance educator who "develops innovative pedagogy in the dance field, groundbreaking teachings that have a significant impact on dance, as well as an established record of exemplary leadership on the state and national level" in the United States.

Lenzu has written for a variety of dance and arts magazines and in 2013 published her first book, entitled *Unveiling Motion and Emotion*. The book, written in both Spanish and English, addresses the importance of dance, community, choreography, and dance pedagogy. Her second book, *Teaching and Learning Dance Through Meaningful Gestures*, explores basic exercises, visualization exercises, active imagination, and artistic application. The book examines how technique is a philosophy and a theory and how the body is an instrument for expression.

In October 2024, Anabella was appointed president of the American Dance Guild, dedicated to supporting artists and bringing the dance community together since 1956. She has also been a board member for the Pioneers Go East Collective since 2021. In the past, she was an advisory board member of Peridance Center, The Brick Theater, and IDACO (Italian Dance Connections Festival) in New York, as well as part of the Host Committee for New Yorkers for Culture and Arts (NY4CA). Anabella served on the Selection Committee for the Bessie's Awards during 2020-2024. She regularly serves on selection panels for national and international grants, residencies, festivals, and other funding organizations.

"The night that you stopped acting/La Noche que dejaste de actuar", Movement Research at Judson Church, 2022

NOTES:

NOTES: